# Showdown at
# ARMAGEDDON

# Showdown at
# ARMAGEDDON

## GEORGE E. VANDEMAN

**Pacific Press Publishing Association**
Boise, Idaho
Oshawa, Ontario, Canada

Edited by Marvin Moore
Designed by Tim Larson
Cover photo by Don Carroll/Image Bank ©
Inside illustrations by Ira Lee
Type set in 10/12.5 Century Schoolbook

The author assumes full responsibility for the accuracy of all facts and quotations cited in this book.

**Library of Congres Catalogue Number: 87-62914**

ISBN 0-8163-0735-0

91 92 • 5 4

# Contents

# Chapter 1

# Jerusalem Invaded

It happened in the early morning of June 5, 1967. Wave upon wave of Israeli bombers swept in from the Mediterranean, flying so low they escaped radar detection. By nightfall the surprise attack had left hundreds of Egyptian war planes lying in ruins.

Israel, threatened with immediate invasion by neighboring nations, had decided to strike first. And they hit hard! By the evening of the second day Israeli fighter jets had crippled the Arab air forces, destroying more than 400 planes while losing just twenty-six of their own. Israeli ground troops won equally stunning victories on all fronts.

Within six days the lightning war was over. The people of Israel, although outnumbered forty to one, vanquished their foes and more than tripled their territory—one of the most brilliant feats in military history. No wonder the Israelis danced in the streets of Jerusalem after that Six-Day War.

From Israel's beginnings in 1948 as an independent nation, its existence has been a series of miracles. Miracles long overdue. For nineteen centuries, the Jewish people had been scattered as aliens throughout the world. Although they enriched their host countries wherever they went, they suffered unrelenting persecution. Then came Hitler's so-called Final Solution—the unspeakable horrors of the Holocaust.

But at last the world community recognized the rights of Jewish people to live safely and freely, governing themselves. With a United Nations mandate as their authority, Jewish colonists fought for independence. They overcame formidable odds to create a new nation in their ancient homeland.

I was there to watch it happen on May 14, 1948. That Friday morning in Jerusalem I stood in front of the King David Hotel. Exactly where I planned to go, I don't remember now. But suddenly a long black limousine pulled up and the door opened. "Going to Convention Hall?" a Jewish gentleman asked.

"Why not?" I thought.

Several important-looking people made room for me, so I slid in beside them. We raced through the narrow streets toward the hurriedly-constructed Convention Hall, where they escorted me inside and seated me with the VIPs. Then I watched the history of the world turn a corner as a new democracy was born in Israel.

Since that memorable day four decades ago, the Middle East has occupied center stage in world affairs. Much more is involved than a struggle between Arabs and Israelis. The world's superpowers have vital interests there which they have pledged to protect at all costs. Many fear that sooner or later World War III will be launched in the Middle East.

A new world war could have happened in 1973. Egypt and Syria rolled their Soviet-built tanks across the border into Israel, vowing revenge for the Six-Day War. They caught their foe completely off guard—it was Yom Kippur, the holiest day of the Jewish year.

But Israel quickly rallied from its setbacks and took the offensive, aided by a massive airlift of supplies from the United States. Meanwhile, behind closed doors the superpowers were edging frighteningly close to a nuclear showdown. As President Nixon recalled later, "[Soviet leader] Brezhnev demanded that the United States join him in sending 'peace-keeping' forces into the Mideast to force a settlement on Israel. We firmly declined and urged diplomatic rather than military action. Brezhnev threatened to intervene unilaterally. When we picked up reports that Soviet forces were embarking on troop transports, we warned Brezhnev that we would not tolerate unilateral intervention and emphasized our determination by putting our conventional and nuclear forces on alert." [1]

Thank God, the Soviets agreed to a diplomatic solution to stop the fighting. Once again Israel's democracy survived, and world war was postponed.

Should all this end-time unrest and upheaval in the Middle East surprise us, or had prophets in the Bible predicted it? Is there any word from the Lord for this crisis hour?

In these pages we will examine what Bible prophecy has in store for the Holy Land. We will also trace the fascinating roots of strife between Arabs and Israelis, going back 4,000 years. You see, this conflict involves more than politics. At its heart is a battle between two ancient religions, both finding their roots in the Old Testament patriarch Abraham.

The Israelis believe God gave Palestine to them through Abraham's son Isaac. Arabs led by Muslim fundamentalists, on the other hand, see themselves as the rightful inheritors of the Promised Land through Abraham's other son Ishmael.

Personally, I feel deeply for both the Israelis and the Arabs. For the Israelis, who quote Old Testament promises that God gave the land to them—and for the Arabs, who have lived in Palestine all these years and now find themselves left out.

As I visited the refugee camps of those displaced Palestinians back in 1948, my heart went out to them. This Arab-Israeli conflict has two sides, you know, and I want this book to present a balanced picture of a very delicate situation there.

We Christians are vitally involved in Middle East events. After all, the Lord Jesus lived and died for us there in Palestine. Furthermore, many believe that the return of Jewish people to Palestine and the establishment of Israel have tremendous spiritual significance. They see in this a fulfillment of Bible prophecy setting the stage for an Armageddon showdown.

Back in the 70s, the largest nonfiction seller for the decade was Hal Lindsey's *The Late Great Planet Earth.* Lindsey predicted that within the span of a generation after 1948—about forty years—Christ would return to this earth secretly and "rapture" His people up to heaven. The unsaved left behind would suffer seven years of tribulation, climaxing in that dreadful battle of Armageddon.

How much of this teaching is Bible truth, and how much is human speculation? Let's examine the prophecies for ourselves. Our study will center on the often-overlooked book of Daniel, which forms the Old Testament foundation for the New Testament book of Revelation. Daniel records the life-and-death struggle between two cities, Jerusalem and Babylon—a preview of events soon to happen in our time. Chapter one opens with Babylon's attack upon Jerusalem six centuries before the time of Christ. It's an intriguing story:

"In the third year of the reign of Jehoiakim king of Judah, Nebuchadnezzar king of Babylon came to Jerusalem and besieged it. And the Lord gave Jehoiakim king of Judah into his hand, with some of the articles of the house of God, . . . and he brought the articles into the treasure house of his god." Daniel 1:1, 2.*

Shocking words indeed. The Lord gave His chosen people into the hand of a pagan power! He even permitted heathen invaders to remove sacred things from His sanctuary and carry them off to Babylon's pagan temple.

Why? Hadn't God promised to defend His people and His temple at all costs, under all circumstances? What had gone wrong?

An even more basic question confronts us here, something you may have wondered about: Why did God have a chosen people in the first place? Does He play favorites?

We must go back to the time of father Abraham to discover why God chose Israel. The promise to Abraham is found in Genesis 12:2, 3:

---

*Unless otherwise indicated, scripture references in this book are from the New King James Version. Emphasis is supplied by the author.

"I will make you a great nation; . . . and you shall be a blessing. . . . In you all the families of the earth shall be blessed."

So God chose Israel to be a blessing to the whole world, a world lost in sin's darkness. Through His chosen nation God wanted to reveal His love to every heathen nation. He hoped they would repent and join with Israel at the banquet of His salvation.

You see, God wasn't playing favorites by having a chosen people. He blessed Abraham for the sake of the Gentiles too. But Abraham's descendants failed to catch the vision. The ancient Israelites squandered divine blessings on themselves, refusing to shine for God as the light of the world.

Worse yet, the Jewish nation came to consider itself Heaven's unique favorite, unconditionally blessed by God. Israel imagined that regardless of how they behaved they would remain the permanent people of God. Thus presuming upon Heaven's mercy, they became careless, even rebellious. Incredibly, they even adopted the idolatry of their neighbors. Immorality abounded in the worship of the sun god Baal, which accommodated a variety of illicit sexual practices. And some Israelite parents actually sacrificed their children on the altars of pagan gods.

God had no choice but to let His people reap the results of their sin. He allowed the heathen nations which they imitated to attack them. In distress the Israelites cried for God to deliver them, and in mercy He saved them again and again. The book of Judges records the sad cycle of apostasy and deliverance, followed by repeated apostasy.

Warning after warning came and went unheeded. God's people even murdered some of His Old Testament messengers. They refused to believe that God would actually employ a heathen power as His instrument to punish them.

But finally judgment day came, and Babylon, the center of pagan worship, invaded Jerusalem in the year 605 B.C. King Nebuchadnezzar eventually sacked and burned the holy city of peace. The glorious temple lay in ruins. Many of the healthy and young who survived the attacks were marched as captives to Babylon, 500 dusty and miserable miles away, near the present site of Baghdad, Iraq.

In every time of trouble God has had a faithful few who remained loyal to Him. The first chapter of Daniel records the exciting story of four young men, probably still teenagers, who stood firmly for God in that heathen land. Daniel and his three friends Hananiah, Mishael, and Azariah caught the eye of Nebuchadnezzar and his officials. They found them to be "young men in whom there was no blemish, but good-looking, gifted in all wisdom, possessing knowledge and quick to understand, who had ability to serve in the king's palace, and whom they might teach the language and literature of the Chaldeans." Daniel 1:4.

These handsome young fellows had it made, there in the palaces of Babylon. I can imagine the young ladies of the city had their eyes on them. So did Nebuchadnezzar himself, who "appointed for them a daily provision of the king's delicacies and of the wine which he drank, and three years of training for them, so that at the end of that time they might serve before the king." Verse 5.

At first it must have seemed like the end of the world to Daniel and his friends when the invaders tore them away from their families and took them captive. But surprise—along came the good life! A scholarship to the University of Babylon and a great government job waiting for them upon graduation, with wine, women, and song along the way.

"But Daniel purposed in his heart that he would not defile himself with the portion of the king's delicacies, nor with the wine which he drank." Verse 8.

Bless his heart. Amid the allurements of the world, Daniel refused to defile himself. He determined to remain faithful to the God who had saved his life. He would honor his Creator by guarding body and soul from the tantalizing temptations of the world. We need more Daniels today, wouldn't you say? With drugs, alcohol, and illicit sex degrading and defiling our youth, we need noble teenagers who will "just say No." "No" to temptation and "Yes" to God's plan for their lives.

Yes, Daniel and his friends determined to be faithful to their God. But Nebuchadnezzar seemed determined to erase every trace of their Hebrew heritage. He even changed their names, calling them after his pagan gods.

Just think how tempting it must have been to abandon their faith. After all, their prayers for God to defend Jerusalem had apparently gone unanswered. And now they found themselves in the center of paganism, with the heathen world opening its arms of opportunity to them.

Why not give up and give in? Evidently their fellow captives from Jerusalem did. But Daniel and his friends didn't.

Soon a further test came along. The king's steward had been charged with the responsibility of keeping the Hebrew captives in good health. Imagining that their simple, natural-foods diet would fail to keep them fit, the steward insisted that Daniel and his friends eat and drink what everybody else indulged in.

With wisdom from heaven, Daniel came up with a proposal:

"Please test your servants for ten days, and let them give us vegetables to eat and water to drink. Then let our countenances be examined before you, and the countenances of the young men who eat the portion of the king's delicacies; and as you see fit, so deal with your servants." Verses 12, 13.

Fair enough, wouldn't you say? The king's steward agreed.

And sure enough, "At the end of ten days their countenance appeared better and fatter in flesh than all the young men who ate the portion of the king's delicacies. Thus the steward took away their portion of delicacies and the wine that they were to drink, and gave them vegetables." Verses 15, 16.

Some Christians today suggest that it doesn't matter what we eat or drink. But Daniel and his friends knew better. And heaven richly blessed their faithfulness:

"As for these four young men, God gave them knowledge and skill in all literature and wisdom; and Daniel had understanding in all visions and dreams." Verse 17.

These visions and dreams which God gave Daniel are the most far-reaching time prophecies in the Bible. Daniel's prophecies have tremendous significance for us now, yet they are usually overlooked or misunderstood by twentieth-century Christians. But in these pages we will study them carefully.

Now back to the story of Daniel and his friends. After their three years of college, Nebuchadnezzar summoned them for their graduation exam. "And in all matters of wisdom and understanding about which the king examined them, he found them ten times better than all the magicians and astrologers who were in all his realm." Verse 20.

Thrilling story! Daniel and his friends remained loyal and true with everyone around them forfeiting faith. We see here a symbol of God's people at the end of time who will "keep the commandments of God and the faith of Jesus." Revelation 14:12.

How about you and me? Will we, like Daniel, purpose in our hearts that we will not permit our bodies and souls to be defiled by sin?

But perhaps you already feel defiled and unholy. Recently a young woman (I'll call her Kathy) contacted me, heartbroken after her live-in boyfriend abandoned her and left town. She felt terribly alone and very guilty. She doubted whether any decent man could want her now. Her life was ruined forever, she feared.

Kathy's guilt-ridden heart craved peace, and she needed power from God to put her life in order. I shared with her good news from the Old Testament gospel prophet:

"We all, like sheep, have gone astray, each of us has turned to his own way; and the Lord has laid on him [Jesus Christ] the iniquity of us all." Isaiah 53:6, NIV.

So we are all guilty, deserving of death. But thank God, Jesus paid it all. On the cross He paid the full price of our sin so that now we can stand clean before God.

Kathy could hardly believe that she could be forgiven so

fully and freely. "And there's more," I told her: "The Lord not only pardons us and counts us holy—He also gives us strength to live a new life for Him. He has a special plan for each of us individually. And as we continue to follow Him, God considers us perfect in Jesus."

Wonderful news! To a woman caught in adultery Jesus said, "Neither do I condemn you." And with the joy of that forgiveness came the power to "go and sin no more." John 8:11.

Will we also come to Jesus and be saved? And then will we live faithfully in loyalty and obedience?

I urge you to open your heart to God just now.

---

1. Richard Nixon, "How to Live With the Bomb," *National Review*, Sept. 20, 1985, pp. 28, 29.

# Chapter 2

# Thunderball From Israel

They dropped out of the midnight sky over Lake Victoria, landed, and coasted silently down the runway toward the Entebbe airport terminal. There in the heart of Africa, more than a hundred Israeli hostages held their breath between life and death.

As the Hercules C-130s rolled to a stop, one of them dropped its tail ramp. Out came a black Mercedes limousine, along with two Land Rovers filled with commandos disguised as Palestinians. In the back of the limousine sat a bulky officer with his face blackened, impersonating the Ugandan dictator Idi Amin.

Now the commando team approached the terminal, led by the black Mercedes. The airport guards snapped to attention and saluted, recognizing Amin's personal license plate (counterfeited by the Israelis). The rescuers moved past the guards toward the hostages.

Inside the terminal, the shooting lasted a minute and forty-five seconds. Then came the triumphant shout of liberation: *"Hanachnu Israelim* [We are Israelis]!"

As the C-130s with their precious cargo lifted off into the friendly skies of freedom, some of the former hostages wept. Others sat in stunned silence. One woman kept crying out, *"Moq Ness! Ness* [A Miracle! A Miracle]!"

And that it certainly was. The Israelis called their mission impossible "Operation Thunderball," after the James Bond thriller. How appropriate that these hostages obtained their

17

freedom on July 4, 1976—the very day of our U.S. bicentennial anniversary. The commandos returned home to be hailed as international heroes.

*Psychology Today* carried a personality profile analyzing the Israeli war heroes.[1] They rated especially high in four areas: leadership, devotion to duty, decisiveness, and perseverance under stress. Certainly the commandos at Entebbe displayed these heroic traits. So did another young Israeli long ago—Daniel, whom we met in our last chapter. His leadership, devotion to duty, and decisiveness set the standard for modern heroes. As for that fourth quality, perseverance under stress—would you believe that *seven decades* after taking his stand for God in Babylon, Daniel was still going strong in the king's service?

Even more remarkable, when Babylon fell to the Medes and Persians, the new king Darius installed the nearly ninety-year-old Daniel as a chief president over his kingdom.

Let's try to imagine a similar scenario. Suppose that some foreign power conquered our nation and then installed the American vice-president as their new prime minister. Incredible—yet this is exactly Daniel's story.

Many terrible things happened to Daniel during his time in Babylon. Crisis after crisis confronted him, yet he fearlessly conquered them all through faith. The Old Testament book by his name contains Daniel's life story plus the amazing prophecies God gave him. You would enjoy reading the book of Daniel.

Come with me now to chapter 9. Let's pay the aged leader a visit to see how he is doing after all those years. We find him quite concerned about something. Let's find out what is going on:

"In the first year of his [King Darius'] reign I, Daniel, understood . . . by the word of the Lord, given through Jeremiah the prophet, that He would accomplish seventy years in the desolations of Jerusalem." Daniel 9:2.

According to prophecy, the Jewish people exiled from

Jerusalem by Babylon would remain in captivity just seventy years. See Jeremiah 25:11, 12. After that time expired, God promised to "bring them up and restore them to this place." Jeremiah 27:22.

But something seemed wrong to Daniel. Even though just two years remained before those seventy years were up, nothing seemed to be happening. Nothing seemed to be in the works that would prepare the way for the exiles to return to Jerusalem. Why not?

Deeply troubled, Daniel brought his problem to God: "Then I set my face toward the Lord God to make request by prayer and supplications, with fasting, sackcloth, and ashes." Daniel 9:3.

Now, why should Daniel be so distressed? God had said seventy years—an open-and-shut promise, right? *Or maybe not!*

There was another factor that Daniel knew about—something beyond God's willingness to keep His promises. You see, the exiles had to fulfill *their* part in the agreement God made with them. We see this revealed in Daniel's prayer:

"I prayed to the Lord my God, and made confession, and said, 'O Lord, great and awesome God, who keeps His covenant and mercy with those who love Him, and with those who keep His commandments.'" Verse 4.

So God keeps His covenant with those who comply with its conditions. Daniel was concerned that, because of their unfaithfulness, the Jewish exiles might not be permitted to return to Jerusalem, even though they were nearly due to return home after the seventy years foretold in Jeremiah's prophecy.

We should remember that any covenant is a partnership, an agreement between two parties, with conditions for both to fulfill. The covenant of marriage is a good example. If you are married, think of the time you walked up the aisle and stood before the minister to exchange vows. The two of you made a covenant together. Both of you agreed to accept its terms—and abide by those terms—or the covenant would be broken.

Just so with the covenant between the Lord and the Jewish nation. More is involved than a dependable God keeping His promises. His people also must abide by the terms of the covenant. *All of God's covenant promises are conditional upon human cooperation.* See Jeremiah 18:7-10.

Let's learn more about this covenant. It's the same everlasting covenant of grace God made with Abraham in Genesis 17. One night He called Abraham to come outside his tent and urged him to look upward toward the desert sky. See the stars? God asked. "So shall your descendants be." Abraham "believed in the Lord, and He accounted it to him for righteousness." Genesis 15:5, 6.

Notice that Abraham's covenant was based on belief, not works. Many think God saved people in Old Testament times through their works, and then in He switched things around in the New Testament and introduced salvation by faith. That wouldn't be fair, would it?

And it's also not true. The gospel of grace runs clear through the Old Testament like a refreshing mountain stream. Even though the Israelites at Mount Sinai wanted a covenant based on works, that did not annul the covenant of grace made with Abraham 430 years previously. See Galatians 3:17.

Picture Abraham and his son Isaac at Mount Moriah, that mountain of sacrifice. The aged father trembles at the thought of losing his son. Then he remembers the gospel: "My son, God will provide for Himself the lamb for a burnt offering." Genesis 22:8.

God Himself provides the sacrifice for sin. That's our assurance today. It was Daniel's hope as well, the promise of the covenant.

But had not the covenant been voided because of the persistent wickedness of God's people? Would the exiles never be allowed to return to their homeland? Daniel feared this was the case.

Then all of a sudden, while Daniel was still praying, the angel Gabriel arrived from heaven with some good news: "O Daniel, I have now come forth to give you skill to understand." Daniel 9:22.

Gabriel proceeded to explain: "Seventy weeks are determined for your people and for your holy city, to finish the transgression, to make an end of sins, to make reconciliation for iniquity, to bring in everlasting righteousness, to seal up vision and prophecy, and to anoint the Most Holy." Verse 24.

Good news indeed—God had not yet disqualified the Jewish nation for their sinfulness. They would return to Jerusalem in fulfillment of Jeremiah's prophecy. And God had determined for them an additional time of national probation—a period of seventy weeks. This would prepare the way for the Messiah, who would "make reconciliation for iniquity" and "bring in everlasting righteousness."

Come with me in your imagination to Calvary that dark Friday afternoon. We see Jesus on the cross, fulfilling His Daniel 9 covenant promise to make atonement for iniquity. With His dying breath He cries, "It is finished!" John 19:30. His mission impossible is accomplished!

Jesus triumphed over sin and brought in everlasting righteousness. Now, through Calvary, we all can find acceptance with God, through faith in His covenant of salvation. This is heaven's remedy for the sin problem that Daniel prayed about.

Every Christian can quickly recognize in Daniel 9 a thrilling forecast of salvation in Christ. But there's more here—a time prophecy indicating exactly when Jesus would appear as the Messiah:

"Know therefore and understand, that from the going forth of the command to restore and build Jerusalem until Messiah the Prince, there shall be seven weeks and sixty-two weeks." Daniel 9:25.

Let's decode this intriguing prophecy—a time span of seven weeks plus sixty-two weeks, totaling sixty-nine weeks.

Jerusalem had been devastated during the Babylonian invasion. The starting point of the sixty-nine-week prophecy would be a special command going forth to rebuild Jerusalem, and the sixty-nine weeks themselves would stretch from that time until the appearance of Jesus, the Messiah.

Fascinating, wouldn't you say? Let's do a quick calculation. Sixty-nine weeks equals a year and a third—483 days to be exact. Strange, you say, it was actually more like 483 *years* from the time Jerusalem was rebuilt until the time of Jesus. And you're right. In fact, it's *exactly 483 years*.

You see, the word translated "weeks" literally means "sevens." And that could be a unit of seven *days* or a unit of seven *years*. As we watch Daniel 9 being fulfilled in history, it becomes evident that we have here a time prophecy with sixty-nine units of seven years each, totaling 483 years, not just days.

Do you follow me? This prophecy foretold that 483 years would separate the time Jerusalem would be rebuilt from the time Messiah would appear.

But did it really happen just like that? Let's find out.

First we must learn the date when the decree actually went forth enabling the Jewish exiles to restore the city of Jerusalem. Fortunately we don't have to guess about that date. The book of Ezra records this decree in the seventh year of the Persian king Artaxerxes, which was 457 B.C. See Ezra 7:8, 11-13.

This date has been confirmed by modern discoveries in archaeology, a fact recognized by many Bible scholars. The widely-acclaimed *Encyclopedia of Bible Difficulties*, for example, endorses the year 457 B.C. as the date for the fulfillment of Daniel 9. This book, recently published by Zondervan, explains how the prophecy unfolds. Notice carefully:

"If, then, the decree of 457 granted to Ezra himself is taken as the . . . commencement of the . . . 483 years, we come out to the precise year of the appearance of Jesus of Nazareth as Messiah (or Christ): 483 minus 457 comes out to A.D. 26. But since a year is gained in passing from 1 B.C. to A.D. 1 (there being no such year as *zero*), it actually comes out to A.D. 27 . . . a most remarkable exactitude in the fulfillment of such an ancient prophecy." [2]

This is mathematical proof that Jesus is the Messiah! In A.D. 27, the very year foretold by Daniel 9, Jesus was anointed as Messiah at His baptism. He went forth announcing that the "time is fulfilled." Mark 1:15.

What time was He talking about? What else but the prophetic time of Daniel 9—the sixty-nine weeks of years that would introduce "Messiah the Prince." This was a prophetic fulfillment of amazing precision! You can see a diagram of all this in the chart below.

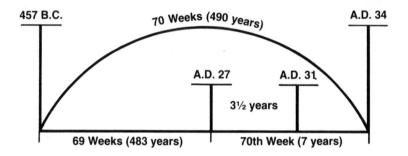

And there's more. You may recall that when Jesus began His miracles, the religious leaders kept trying to put Him to death. But again and again Christ escaped. One such episode is recorded in John 7:30:

"They sought to take Him; but no one laid a hand on Him, because *His hour had not yet come.*"

This suggests that perhaps there was a special date set for Christ to die. Was this also foretold in Bible prophecy? Prophecy gives us the date A.D. 27 when He was anointed as the Messiah. Does it also tell us of the three-and-a-half-year period of His ministry?

Notice another bit of information: The evening before He died Jesus prayed, "Father, *the hour has come.*" John 17:1. Evidently there was a calendar countdown to Calvary! And, indeed, Jesus died for our sins at exactly the time foretold by Daniel 9—right in the middle of an *additional* week of years beyond the original sixty-nine weeks which led up to His baptism. Notice:

"In the *middle of the week* He shall bring an end to sacrifice and offering." Daniel 9:27.

The middle of that seventieth week of seven years, of course, would be three and a half years after Jesus began His ministry. And that's exactly when He ended the age of sacrifices and sin offerings by His death. The veil of the temple was torn in two, showing that there was no further need for the Jewish temple services.

So Calvary took place right on schedule in A.D. 31, three and a half years after Christ's baptism. This is proof positive that Jesus is exactly who He claimed to be—the Messiah, the Lamb of God! Is it any wonder that thousands of Jewish people today have sealed their faith in Jesus as Messiah through this calendar countdown in Daniel 9?

It's interesting that Jesus chose the number "seventy times seven" to illustrate how long we should have mercy on those who hurt us. Did He have in mind Daniel's time prophecy of "seventy times seven," those years of God's mercy for the nation of Israel? We don't know. But it's something to think about.

Now back to Daniel 9. The last week of years in the prophecy—this seventieth week—did not end with the crucifixion of Christ. Three and a half additional years remained after the "middle of the week." This takes us from the time of Calvary in the spring of A.D. 31 down to A.D. 34, the end of those "seventy weeks" of probation given to the Jewish nation in Daniel 9:24.

So God kept His promise in the covenant and sent Jesus as the Messiah. How did the Jewish people respond after the

Messiah died in A.D. 31? How did they spend the last three and a half years remaining in the time granted by the covenant?

This question is crucial. *Any covenant must be honored by both partners in order for it to remain effective.* So the covenant God made with the Jewish nation required their cooperation, their faith in the Messiah.

Let's go back to 1978 and the Camp David covenant, no doubt the landmark accomplishment of President Carter's administration. He managed to get Menahem Begin of Israel and Anwar Sadat of Egypt to sit down together for nearly two weeks, discussing peace in the Middle East. After long hours of painstaking negotiation and skilled diplomacy by our President, Begin and Sadat agreed to that historic peace accord finally signed at the White House.

In order for that covenant of peace to be preserved, continuing compliance by both Egypt and Israel is necessary. That's because a covenant is always a partnership affair—either party has the power to break the covenant.

*So it is with God's covenant.* It is a covenant of grace, to be sure, completely undeserved—but we have a part in it. We must accept it and live by its terms of faith in the Messiah. *To suggest that this covenant could be fulfilled without faith in the Messiah would be to deny the agreement God made with Abraham.*

The apostle Paul in Galatians put it so plainly, "So then *those who are of faith* are blessed with believing Abraham." Galatians 3:9. *"If you are Christ's,* then you are Abraham's seed, and heirs according to the promise." Verse 29.

Outside of faith in the Messiah, God's covenant cannot be fulfilled. We must nail that down and never forget it.

Now let's visit Entebbe again and review Operation Thunderball one more time. The first of the rescuers off the plane and the last one safely back on board was Brigadier General Dan Shomron. This thirty-nine-year-old hero of heroes received an avalanche of adoring letters from around the world. Hundreds of gifts also arrived—all of which he promptly returned.

"I don't understand all the fuss," General Shomron shrugged. "I am only one of many anonymous fighters."

But his modesty overlooked his long history of valor. During the Six-Day War his paratroop battalion was the first Israeli unit to reach the Suez Canal, and in the Yom Kippur fighting his armored brigade knocked out sixty Egyptian tanks. A distinguished record indeed for one of such humility, wouldn't you say?

But genuine humility is a characteristic of many Israeli war heroes. That *Psychology Today* profile I mentioned earlier in this chapter revealed that many of the medal winners doubted "whether they had been more worthy of the medals than some of their peers in the same unit." Imagine!

This humility of the Israeli heroes was also seen in the life of ancient Daniel. In that prayer of chapter 9—one of the most heart-touching in all the Bible—you might have been surprised that he confessed *his* sinfulness along with that of his people: "We have sinned," he said, and "we have done wickedly." Daniel 9:15.

What was Daniel talking about, confessing himself as a sinner? We have no record of Daniel ever yielding to sin, although I'm sure he had his weak moments. But even his jealous enemies could find no improprieties in his conduct. See Daniel 6:4.

So at first we might be astonished that Daniel offered such a prayer. Then we recall the words of the prophet Isaiah: "We are all like an unclean thing, and all our righteousnesses are like filthy rags." Isaiah 64:6.

Even though I'm sure Daniel had nothing in particular to repent of, he knew he still failed to reach God's glorious ideal. And so he confessed himself to be a fellow sinner in a community that needed a Messiah.

Notice what Daniel's hope of salvation was: "We do not present our supplications before You because of our righteous deeds, but because of Your great mercies. O Lord, hear! O Lord, forgive!" Daniel 9:18, 19.

Daniel put his hope in salvation by grace. And nothing but heaven's pure mercy will ever qualify us for heaven. As we prepare for earth's final showdown at Armageddon, may God help us all to live by faith in the Lord Jesus Christ.

---

1. Jack C. Horn, "A Call to Glory," *Psychology Today*, December 1985, p. 20.

2. Gleason L. Archer, *Encyclopedia of Bible Difficulties* (Grand Rapids, Mich: Zondervan Publishing House, 1982), pp. 290, 291.

# Chapter 3
# The Mystique of Islam

Missiles to Iran. Undercover aid to the Contras. Secret Swiss bank accounts and payoffs to shadowy arms merchants.

Some pundits suggest that the Iran-Contra affair was more complex than any plot Hollywood could invent. The revelations of international intrigue amazed everyday Americans and veteran members of Congress alike.

Nothing seemed more bizarre than the sight of that Iranian official waving a leather-bound Bible in front of the cameras. Who could forget his triumphant smile as he announced that the Bible had been a gift from President Reagan.

At first the White House discounted the report, but later the President's spokesman confirmed it. In October of 1986 President Reagan had indeed sent the Bible as a token of good will. There in the Oval Office, before signing his name, he inscribed the following verse from the apostle Paul:

"The Scripture, foreseeing that God would justify the nations by faith, preached the gospel to Abraham beforehand, saying, 'In you all the nations shall be blessed.'" Galatians 3:8.

What did our President mean by quoting this verse? He was reminding the Iranians that all of us, as the descendants of Abraham, are children of God together. President Reagan wanted desperately to reach the hearts of the Iranian leaders, out of his concern for our hostages.

Our leaders might have done things differently had they

foreseen how the Iran initiative would backfire, but surely we all can appreciate their desire to achieve understanding among the Muslim, Christian, and Jewish people.

Although it may seem hard to believe, all three religions share the same ancestor in Abraham. And each group was represented at Camp David during the peace talks in 1978. Egyptian leader Sadat was a Muslim, the Israeli Prime Minister Begin was Jewish, and our President Carter represented Christianity.

Occasionally at Camp David the leaders found themselves discussing religion. President Carter, in his book *The Blood of Abraham,*[1] recalled that Sadat seemed especially eager for spiritual dialogue. Often the Arab leader mentioned his plans for building a shrine on Mount Sinai so that believers of all three religions could worship together. Sadat expressed delight that Muslims, Jews, and Christians all shared the same blood of Abraham. Begin appeared somewhat embarrassed at this thought, Carter observed.

So all three religions claim the same father in Abraham. Many Americans are curious about Islam, the belief of the Muslims. We hear on the news about terrorists committing horrible crimes against innocent hostages for the sake of their holy war, and we wonder what kind of religion Islam must be to condone such atrocities.

It might come as a surprise to you that religious tolerance for Christians and Jews is a basic principle of Islam. Mohammed, pioneer of the Muslims, defended the rights of Christians and Jews to quietly believe as they wished. Of course, sharing the gospel in Muslim lands has always been a challenging undertaking.

Mohammed was born late in the sixth century in the city of Mecca, an important trading center of western Arabia. While in his twenties he found employment with a rich widow, and before long they were married. About the age of forty, Mohammed had a vision in which he believed God called him to present a special message to the world. His religious movement was carried by the sword of the Arabs throughout the Middle East and into Europe.

Thousands of Christians became Muslims almost overnight. Islam spread north into the Alps, maintaining a foothold in Switzerland until the tenth century. If the Arab forces had not been defeated in the Battle of Tours by Charles Martel in 732, all Europe might have become Muslim. No wonder the church in the Middle Ages feared Islam almost as much as we in the twentieth century dread nuclear war!

Today there are almost 800 million Muslims in more than seventy countries, including all the nations that surround Israel. Many Muslims never leave their homes without taking along their scriptures, the Koran. Muslims worship Allah as the only God and honor Mohammed as His prophet. They bow together for prayer five times a day. They also fast between sunrise and sunset for an entire month each year, and they avoid gambling, liquor, and pork.

Evidently Muslims take their religion seriously. In fact, the word *Islam* itself means "entire submission to Allah." Muslims honor Abraham, whom they call *Ibrahim,* as their founding father who set the example for obedience and uncompromising commitment.

What do Muslims think of Jesus Christ? They accept Him as a prophet and teacher, but not as the Son of God and Saviour from sin. Like so many devout but mistaken people around the world, they believe they can save themselves by their good works.

Since Muslims reject Jesus as Messiah, do they have the right to consider themselves Heaven's chosen people? Because they have the blood of Abraham, can Muslims claim him as their spiritual father?

And what about Jewish people who also reject Jesus as Messiah? They don't even honor Him as a prophet as the Muslims do. Can Israelis today consider themselves God's chosen people through the blood of Abraham—while rejecting the blood of Christ?

These are thought-provoking questions, wouldn't you say? Muslims, Jews, and Christians all honor the same spiritual father. Do we all have equal claims on Abraham?

To find out we must go back 4,000 years and explore the roots of our religion. We learn that Abraham's original name was Abram, and his wife's name was Sarai. They lived in Ur of the Chaldees, near where the Euphrates River runs into the Persian Gulf in what is now Iraq. God called them out of their homeland, promising to bless them both as parents of a great nation.

By faith Abram and Sarai obeyed the Lord's call, moving from place to place before finally settling in Canaan. This area between the Jordan River and the Mediterranean Sea was the land promised by God to the patriarch and his descendants. But the seventy-five-year-old Abram still had no children, and Sarai herself was a senior citizen of sixty-five. The elderly couple seemingly had no earthly chance of ever becoming parents.

After further years of waiting they decided to take matters into their own hands outside of God's will. Sarai herself came up with the idea: Why not take her maid Hagar and have a child by her? Abram agreed. Hagar bore him Ishmael, who Muslims honor as their ancestor. But God refused to recognize Hagar's son as the inheritor of the promise made to Abram through Sarai.

Thirteen additional years passed after the birth of Ishmael. Finally the time came to fulfill the covenant. That was the night the Lord called Abram to come outside his tent and urged him to look up at the stars in the desert sky. "So shall your descendants be," God promised.

Then the Lord told Abraham something even more unexpected: "No longer shall your name be called Abram, but your name shall be Abraham; for *I have made you a father* of many nations." Genesis 17:5. Sarai's name God changed to Sarah, which meant "mother of many nations." See verses 15, 16.

Well, it took some faith for Abraham and Sarah to accept

their new names. How could a man one hundred years old and his childless wife of ninety consider themselves already the parents of many nations? Humanly speaking, the idea was foolish—so ridiculous, in fact, that Abraham "fell on his face and laughed" (verse 17) right there in the presence of God. Imagine!

Eventually Abraham and Sarah grasped God's promise, and their faith was counted as righteousness. Notice that God had already declared them to be parents—something they were not. Something they were completely unworthy of considering themselves to be. But by faith they accepted their new names anyway, even though what God called them did not represent what they actually were.

Through this experience of Abraham and Sarah we can understand the faith required by the covenant. Saving faith involves accepting God's declaration of something we are not. You see, when we repent and believe, the Lord counts us perfect through the blood of Christ, even though we are unworthy and unholy.

But notice that faith did bear fruit for Abraham and Sarah. Before long Isaac was born, the miracle child of the covenant. And just as faith worked miracles for Abraham and Sarah, faith in Christ will work miracles in transformed lives today.

Alcoholics become sober through God's grace. Adulterers become trustworthy spouses. Proud legalists become humble and happy believers.

So now we have the background behind three religions— Judaism, Islam, and Christianity. God established His covenant with Abraham through Sarah. Their son Isaac was the faith-child through whom the covenant was fulfilled. Ishmael, the child of the flesh, was born outside of this covenant of faith.

In the truest sense, *Ishmael was not a son of Abraham*. You see, he was born, not to Abraham, but to *Abram*—thirteen years before the patriarch's name was changed to Abraham on the basis of faith.

So Islam, descending from Ishmael, was disqualified from Abraham's covenant right from the start. And Muslims today, despite their high moral principles, still lack the faith principle necessary to fulfill the covenant. Although Islam teaches surrender and commitment, it rejects the gospel. The only hope for Muslims to become true children of Abraham is by sharing his faith, faith in the Messiah of the covenant.

What about the Jewish people? Can they rightly claim Abraham as their spiritual father?

This question came up back in Christ's day. The Pharisees felt no need of Jesus, claiming to be already secure in God's favor as children of Abraham. But Jesus responded, "If you were Abraham's children, you would do the works of Abraham." John 8:39.

Evidently having the blood of Abraham is not enough—Jewish people must obey in covenant faith as Abraham did. But what did God's chosen people do with their Messiah? Unfortunately, "His own received Him not." The nation of Israel crucified its Messiah.

Still God's mercy lingered. The resurrected Christ sent His apostles first to the lost sheep of the house of Israel. This was because the Jewish nation still had left to them three and a half years of national probation. (Remember that time prophecy in Daniel 9.) But those 490 years of opportunity to accept the covenant would expire in A.D. 34.

What did Israel do with its final years of grace? Thousands of individual Israelites accepted Jesus, but the nation itself sealed its rejection of the covenant. After stoning God's messenger Stephen, they launched a great persecution against anyone who believed in Jesus.

At this point the apostles declared, "It was necessary that the word of God should be spoken to you first; but since you reject it, and judge yourselves unworthy of everlasting life, behold, we turn to the Gentiles." Acts 13:46.

Jesus had warned the Jewish leaders that this would happen: "The kingdom of God will be taken from you and given to a nation bearing the fruits of it." Matthew 21:43. Accordingly, the covenant promises were now taken away from the nation of Israel and given to the Christian church.

Of course, Jewish people are still welcome to accept Jesus as their Messiah. Thousands have already done so, and multitudes more will, according to Bible prophecy. But Abraham's covenant now belongs not to one particular nation, but to individual Jewish and Gentile believers: "If you are Christ's, then you are Abraham's seed, and heirs according to the promise." Galatians 3:29. See also Ephesians 2:13-19 and 1 Peter 2:9, 10.

All those who reject faith in the Messiah of the covenant disqualify themselves as the spiritual children of Abraham. They are really children of the flesh, children of *Abram* along with Ishmael. We must share the *faith* of Abraham—not his *blood*—to be the people of the covenant today.

What is the spiritual condition of Israel now? Former President Jimmy Carter recounts his 1973 trip to Israel in that fascinating book he wrote, *The Blood of Abraham*. He tells of visiting several kibbutzim, or Jewish settlements, near the Sea of Galilee. One Sabbath he dropped in on the local synagogue in a community of several hundred and was shocked to find only two other worshipers present.

Later, when the Carters visited Prime Minister Golda Meir, the conversation drifted into religion. Carter commented about the general lack of spiritual interest among the Israelis. The prime minister agreed with his observation, but said she wasn't concerned because of the Orthodox Jews around. She added with a laugh, "If you attend a session of the Knesset [the Israeli parliament], you will see them in action and will know they have not lost their faith."

Well, certainly the Orthodox Jews of Israel today have not lost their zeal. But would we want to call it faith? Faith in the Messiah of the covenant?

If you rented a car and drove through the ultra-Orthodox sections of Jerusalem on the Sabbath, it could be hazardous to your health. The residents there have a habit of throwing rocks at cars, whose drivers they judge to be breaking God's holy day. And we remember that 2,000 years ago zealous sabbatarians in that same city crucified Jesus Christ.

You know what happened. Jesus proclaimed Himself Lord of the Sabbath. See Matthew 12:8. But religious tradition had shackled the Sabbath with so many burdensome requirements that Christ found Himself in continual controversy over the way He honored the Sabbath. See Mark 3:46.

This dispute over the Sabbath climaxed at the cross. Had the Jewish leaders understood the meaning of Sabbath rest, they would not have crucified the Lord of the Sabbath. You see, the seventh day points us to worship Jesus as the Creator and Saviour of the human race.

Back at the beginning of this world, God finished creation in six days and rested the seventh. Then He invited His children to share the celebration of His work—even though they had done nothing to earn the right to rest. They accepted God's accomplishment on their behalf, resting with Him as if they had performed the work themselves.

This Sabbath rest in God's finished work symbolizes what Christianity stands for. Other world religions, including Islam and today's Judaism, focus upon human works—what we can do to achieve our own salvation. But Christians celebrate God's work on our behalf. That's why the Sabbath points us away from our accomplishments, in the same way that Abraham in faith looked outside of himself to receive the covenant. So week by week the Sabbath keeps us resting in Christ through covenant faith.

There's a lesson we can learn from the Jewish nation in Christ's day: religious zeal cannot qualify us for salvation. Morality without covenant faith amounts to legalism. We must sadly conclude that not much has changed in Israel since the day Jesus wept over unrepentant Jerusalem and pronounced that fearful sentence, "Your house is left to you desolate." Matthew 23:38.

Many Christians today eagerly point to the nation of Israel as a divine miracle. They think they see the hand of God fulfilling His covenant there. But consider Islam, the world's fastest-growing religious force. Would we dare suggest that the "miraculous" rise of Islam is evidence of a "divine blessing" upon Muslims?

Perhaps we should take a second look at the situation in Israel. It's not exactly a land flowing with milk and honey—peace and prosperity are strangers there. Israel has been struggling with inflation rates of several hundred percent. And since its beginning in 1948 the nation has suffered an almost constant state of war. Without a massive and continuous dole of American dollars, Israel would probably not survive.

Something is clearly wrong—God does not fight for the Israelis the way He did in Old Testament times.

More serious than anything else in Israel is the religious attitude. Converts to Christ are treated as traitors or even persecuted! The government discourages evangelism.

But somehow American Christians fail to feel much concern. Have we become blinded by pro-Israeli politics?

According to the editor of *Evangelical Missions Quarterly*, "It is dangerously possible to be so enamored with the land [of Israel], and to be so taken up with Israel's cause, that one can forget the desperate spiritual blindness engulfing Israel today."[2]

When most American church leaders travel over there, they show little interest in the spiritual condition of Israel, and they ignore or even avoid the handful of struggling believers there. Why? Surely something is wrong with the popular understanding of Bible prophecy.

Somehow we must come to realize that the hope of Israel today is not in military exploits, nor is it in rebuilding their lost temple to prepare for a showdown at Armageddon. Their only hope lies in repentance and faith in their Messiah. And the same salvation in Jesus Christ is equally available to Muslims, Buddhists, Communists, and everyone else—all of us!

Tell me, friend, have you made your personal commitment to accept Jesus as your Saviour and follow Him as your Lord? Christ's peace in your heart will change your life. The same power of covenant faith that transformed Abraham and Sarah will work miracles in bringing you victory over sin.

The story is told of a new Christian whose faith in the Bible was challenged by his former drinking buddies. "We don't believe Jesus really turned water into wine," they scoffed. "How do you know such a miracle really happened?"

For a moment the new believer wondered what to say. Then he quietly replied, "I admit I can't prove Jesus turned water into wine 2,000 years ago. But I can tell you this. In our home He turned my six-packs of beer into furniture for my family!"

Praise God, He can work miracles in your heart and in your home too.

---

1. Jimmy Carter, *The Blood of Abraham* (New York: Houghton Mifflin, 1985), pp. 8, 9.

2. Cited by Byron Spradlin in "We Can Love Israel Too Much," *Christianity Today*, July 10, 1987, p. 14.

# Chapter 4

# Massacre in the Church

A group of children, led by twelve-year-old Nicholas, departed Europe for the Mediterranean. They weren't going off to summer camp. These young people had been recruited as Christian soldiers to march in a holy war against the Muslims.

It happened long ago, in the year 1212. The children's army planned to actually cross the sea on dry land and recapture the tomb of Christ in Jerusalem.[1]

They never made it to Palestine. Thousands died from disease along the way or were sold as slaves.

Who commissioned this tragic Children's Crusade?

To get the background we must go to the late seventh century, shortly after the death of Mohammed. Muslim armies embarked on a quest for territory unlike anything the world had seen since Alexander the Great. Jerusalem fell to Islamic rule along with the entire Holy Land. Christian pilgrimages to Palestine became risky and eventually impossible.

Four centuries of Muslim occupation passed. Then in 1095 Pope Urban II decided it was time to take action and win back the Holy Land by force. He declared war upon the Muslims by launching a crusade, the first in a series of Christian military expeditions.

In that First Crusade, armies of the church regained Jerusalem on July 15, 1099. It was a savage battle. The Christian invaders plunged their swords into every Muslim and even every Jewish person they found inside the city.[2] Observers reported that the soldiers waded in blood, and the slaughter was as horrible as could be imagined. All this in the name of Jesus.

The crusaders managed to maintain control of Jerusalem for a few decades before Muslim forces took the city again. So the church sponsored additional expeditions, including the infamous Children's Crusade.

Finally Rome, caught up in the spirit of holy war, turned its sword against Christian "heretics" in Europe. During those dark centuries, fearful crusades brought wrath upon the Albigenses in southern France and other Christian nonconformists. Many thousands died for their beliefs by being hung, drowned, or burned alive. The record of history is open for all to read.

The darkest hour of the church came the night of August 23, 1572. A bell tolling in the middle of the night signaled the start of the Massacre of Saint Bartholomew in France. Soldiers dragged unsuspecting Protestants from their beds and murdered them.

For days the carnage continued in Paris and the surrounding provinces. Noble and peasant, old and young, mother and child spilled their blood together. Only heaven knows how many perished in this medieval holocaust—as many as 70,000, according to some sources.[3]

When news of the bloodbath reached Rome, the city erupted in celebration. Church bells rang. The cannon of St. Angelo thundered a salute. Pope Gregory XIII had a medallion minted to commemorate the horrors of the massacre.

Catholics today regret those tragic events. We all must resist condemning medieval church leaders for these atrocities. How much better to pray with Christ, "Father forgive them, for they know not what they do."

Indeed, the church of that time believed that persecuting heretics preserved the purity of society. Thomas Aquinas, premier theologian of the Middle Ages, argued that killing heretics saved thousands from following them into eternal torment. Even the rebels themselves might repent through fear of being burned alive. Such was the thinking of the day.[4]

So persecution came in the name of the cross of Christ. Interestingly, the word *crusade* comes from the Latin word for *cross*. Crusaders wore a red cloth cross sewn on their tunics to show that they were Christian soldiers. The medieval church believed that carrying the cross of Christ meant killing nonconformists.

But is the cross of Jesus a sword? Our Lord never led an army. In the Garden of Gethsemane He told Peter to put the sword away. Jesus then warned that those who take up the sword would perish by the sword.

Evidently the medieval church had lost sight of true Christianity. Pure gospel faith became buried beneath tradition, legalism, and a persecution policy. The church through its use of force and fear violated God's covenant of grace.

Back in the first century the Christian church received a warning: "Because of unbelief they [the Jewish nation] were broken off, and you stand by faith. Do not be haughty, but fear. For if God did not spare the natural branches, He may not spare you either." Romans 11:20, 21. The next verse repeats the solemn advice and concludes, "Otherwise you also will be cut off."

The message was clear—the church must fulfill the covenant, or it would be cut off just as the Jewish nation had been. But history was repeating itself. What had happened to Israel now recurred in the Christian church. Once again God's people transgressed His covenant.

The Lord in mercy sent messengers to reform the church, as He had sent prophets to save the Jewish nation. Foremost among the many God sent was Martin Luther.

Luther struggled with a tortured conscience in his early years as an obedient and fervent monk. He pursued purity by depriving himself of life's comforts and necessities.

But nothing he did brought him peace. He could never be

certain he had satisfied God. Finally he learned that the salvation he tried so hard to obtain, Christ offered as a gift. The truth which set him free came from the New Testament book of Romans. Chapter 3 explains how God Himself took the punishment we sinners deserve, so we can be freely forgiven in the Lord Jesus Christ.

Luther could hardly believe this good news. Despite his guilt he could be credited with holiness—because Jesus, who really was holy, suffered his penalty.

Of course, Rome had always pointed sinners to come to God (through the church) for salvation. But Luther introduced a vital new dimension: He discovered that believers, even though sinful, can at the same time be counted righteous. You see, God considers sinners to be saints as soon as they trust in Jesus—even before their lives reveal good works (which, of course, will be forthcoming).

Luther discovered this wonderful truth in Romans 4:5. Notice what this verse says: "To him who does not work but believes on Him who justifies the ungodly, his faith is accounted for righteousness."

So the ungodly who surrender to Jesus are justified. Forgiveness comes, not because we are holy, nor by works, Luther now realized, but because we trust in Jesus.

Joy and peace filled the Reformer's heart. But the gospel that soothed his own soul aroused conflict with Rome. Luther, convinced that the church interfered with people's personal relationship with God, proclaimed Jesus to be the only Mediator between heaven and earth. He proclaimed that "the true Christian pilgrimage is not to Rome . . . but to the prophets, the Psalms and the Gospels."

The Reformer's growing understanding of Bible truth raised doubts about purgatory after death. "If the pope does have power to release anyone from purgatory," he challenged, "why in the name of love does he not abolish purgatory by letting everyone out?"

As you can well imagine, Luther found himself increasingly alienated from Rome. The separation became final when he condemned the church as antichrist. Pope Leo X responded by excommunicating Luther on January 3, 1521. His writings were banned and burned. The reformer himself seemed bound to be burned at the stake.

In the twentieth century, things have calmed down in Christianity. Protestants and Catholics don't battle one another as much as before. We certainly thank God for the spirit of good will we find among us today.

But a disturbing question confronts us: Have we truly resolved the issues of the Reformation? Christians today tend to dismiss the bold statements of Martin Luther as overheated rhetoric from the distant past. But perhaps we should again look at the painstaking scholarship which compelled Luther to proclaim such unpopular and life-threatening truths.

Actually, quite a few scholars in the Middle Ages taught that the church, through its abuse of the Christian faith, had made itself the antichrist. All the major Reformers shared Luther's conclusions, including John Knox of Scotland. So did King James I (who commissioned the translation of our King James Bible), along with the famous scientist and Bible student Sir Isaac Newton. Various men at different times reached the same conclusion.[5]

Most Christians today have abandoned the prophetic heritage of the Reformers. We would do well to recall what the apostle Paul taught about the antichrist: "Let no one deceive you by any means; for that Day [the second coming of Christ] will not come unless the falling away comes first, and the man of sin is revealed, the son of perdition." 2 Thessalonians 2:3.

This "man of sin" is understood by Christians everywhere as the antichrist. And notice: The word *anti* in *antichrist* can mean either "against" or "instead of." In other words, the antichrist power might put itself in the place of Christ rather than openly denying Him.

Which of these two approaches would the antichrist use?

The apostle warned, "Let no man deceive you." The antichrist power would emerge amid deception, amid a "falling away" *within the church.* The antichrist arises out of an apostasy within Christianity. This is deception, you see, not an open attack upon faith in Christ.

So the great antichrist power would be born and raised in the heart of Christianity. Shocking indeed, but didn't Jesus warn about deception? A wolf in sheep's clothing!

The church itself becoming the antichrist power—what could be more deceptive, more unexpected in setting the stage for Armageddon! That's just what the Reformers realized as they pointed their fearless fingers toward Rome.

Were they all mistaken? Or did they discover something we have overlooked?

Many Christians are curious to know what it was that convinced the Reformers about the antichrist. It might be interesting to open our Bibles to Daniel 7 and find out. We find in this chapter a prophecy concerning four beasts. Verse 23 explains that "the fourth beast shall be a fourth kingdom on earth, which shall be different from all other kingdoms."

Scholars agree that the four kingdoms of Daniel 7 are Babylon, Greece, Persia, and Rome. And this text predicted that the fourth kingdom, the Roman Empire, would be different from the other three. Rather than giving way to another single world power, Rome would be followed by ten kingdoms. Notice: "The ten horns are ten kings who shall arise from this kingdom. And another shall arise after them; he shall be different from the first ones, and shall subdue three kings." Daniel 7:24.

Did the Roman empire indeed collapse into ten kingdoms? Yes. Modern Europe descended from ten Germanic tribes which followed the Roman Empire. And our text predicted that three of those tribes would be subdued by a new power— which the Reformers identified as the church headquartered in Rome.

Were they correct in their conclusion? Did a religious power in Rome succeed the Roman Empire? History confirms it. In the year 330 Emperor Constantine moved his palace east to Constantinople (now Istanbul), leaving the pontiff in charge at Rome.

A popular college textbook certifies this transfer of power from the Roman Empire to the Roman church: "In the West, the Church took over the defense of Roman civilization. The emperor gave up the [pagan] title of Pontifex Maximus (high priest) because the Roman gods were no longer worshipped. The bishop of Rome assumed these priestly functions, and this is why the Pope today is sometimes referred to as the Pontiff. . . . *The Roman Empire had become the Christian Church.*" [6]

In 533 the Emperor Justinian officially declared the pope to be "head of all the holy churches." In harmony with this declaration he waged war on anyone who refused to honor the authority of the church. Three of the ten tribes—the Heruli, the Ostrogoths, and the Vandals—refused to submit to the papacy. But in March of 538 the last of those rebel tribes fell, and the pope reigned supreme over Christendom.

Ten kingdoms followed Rome. And three of them fell to make way for the papacy. Just a coincidence, or a striking fulfillment of prophecy?

Daniel 7 went on to predict that "he shall speak pompous words against the Most High, shall persecute the saints of the Most High, and shall intend to change times and law. Then the saints shall be given into his hand for a time and times and half a time." Verse 25.

Did these things really happen in the church? Let's consider those four identifying marks one by one:

### 1. "He shall speak pompous words against the Most High."

The church claimed authority to dispense God's forgiveness. For example, in 1076 Pope Gregory VII declared that the citizens of Germany need not obey their king until he submitted to papal authority. Henry IV, the most powerful monarch in Europe, hurried over the wintery Alps to Canossa, where the pontiff was residing. There he waited three days, barefoot in the snow, until the pope finally forgave him.

A remarkable encounter between church and state, wouldn't you say? The medieval popes claimed complete authority over personal conscience. In the late nineteenth century Pope Leo VII commanded "complete submission and obedience of will to the Church and to the Roman Pontiff, as to God Himself."[7] Four years later he made the bold claim: "We [the popes] hold upon this earth the place of God Almighty."[8]

It is not for us to question anyone's sincerity. But requiring allegiance due to God alone ventures onto dangerous ground, wouldn't you say?

### 2. He "shall persecute the saints of the Most High."

The church today frankly acknowledges its history of persecution. According to the *New Catholic Encyclopedia*, "In 1252 [Pope] Innocent IV sanctioned the infliction of torture by the civil authorities upon heretics, and torture later came to have a recognized place in the procedure of the inquisitorial courts."[9]

The same source recognizes that "judged by contemporary standards, the Inquisition, especially as it developed in Spain toward the close of the Middle Ages, can be classified only as one of the darker chapters in the history of the Church."[10]

### 3. He "shall intend to change times and law."

Has the church attempted to change the Ten Commandments, especially in regard to time?

Around the year 1400 Petrus de Ancharano declared that "the pope can modify divine law, since his power is not of man, but of God, and he acts in the place of God upon earth."[11] Luther disputed this teaching of the church. In the Reformer's famous debate with the papal representative Johann Eck, he affirmed that no church tradition would rule his life. Only the Holy Scriptures had control over his conscience.

But Dr. Eck had a card up his sleeve. He called Luther to account for keeping Sunday in place of the Bible Sabbath. Here is his challenge to the Reformer: "Scripture teaches, 'Remember to hallow the Sabbath day; six days shall you labor and do all your work, but the seventh day is the Sabbath day of the Lord your God,' etc. Yet the church has changed the Sabbath into Sunday on its own authority, on which you have no Scripture." [12]

Eck had a point which Luther could not deny. In his battle against church tradition the Reformer had not yet come to grips with the Sabbath question.

Church scholars today repeat Eck's contention. John A. O'Brien asks in his current best-seller (1977), *The Faith of Millions*: "Since Saturday, not Sunday, is specified in the Bible, isn't it curious that non-Catholics who profess to take their religion directly from the Bible and not from the Church, observe Sunday instead of Saturday? . . . That observance remains as a reminder of the Mother Church from which the non-Catholic sects broke away—like a boy running away from home but still carrying in his pocket a picture of his mother or a lock of her hair." [13] Perhaps Protestants ought to ask themselves why they keep Sunday, since obviously tradition accounts for its origin. Something to think about, isn't it? In case you want to investigate this Sabbath question further, I'll be glad to send you my book *When God Made Rest*.

So in the matter of Sabbath versus Sunday we see that the church fulfills Daniel 7 by claiming authority to change "times and laws." Now, one last point remains before we can positively identify the medieval antichrist power:

### 4. "The saints shall be given into his hand for a time and times and half a time."

What prophetic time span do we have here? The Reformers understood these three and a half times to represent 1260 years of papal authority. How did they figure this? They noticed that this same time span is mentioned three times in

Revelation. It is mentioned exactly as Daniel has it (time, times, and half a time) in chapter 12:14. In chapter 12:6 it is spoken of as 1260 days, and in chapter 13:5 it is referred to as forty-two months.

Are these 1260 days literal or symbolic? Remember that in Bible prophecy short-lived beasts symbolize centuries of government. So a much longer time span than 1260 literal days is called for. The answer comes when we realize that in symbolic prophecy a day represents a year. See Ezekiel 4:6.

Now we can see why the Reformers interpreted these 1260 days as 1260 years. As far back as the late twelfth century the Catholic scholar Joachim of Floris, summoned to answer charges of heresy, declared that these 1260 days represented 1260 years of power in the church.[14] And way back in the ninth century several students of the Word believed the same.[15]

History confirms their scholarship. Remember 538, the year when the last rebel tribe was crushed? Is it a mere coincidence that exactly 1260 years later, in 1798, Napoleon's army stormed the Vatican, dethroned Pope Pius IV, and forced him into exile, where he died? I think not. The long medieval reign of the Papacy had come to an end in a most remarkable fulfillment of Bible prophecy!

We can see from our study in Daniel 7 why the Reformers came to their conclusion about the antichrist power. Yet, while we may find their scholarship compelling, we must be careful to be fair. Remember that since the early centuries the term *catholic* applied to all mainstream Christianity—it simply meant the "universal" body of Christ on earth. So in one sense all of us have a "catholic" background.

Here's something else to consider. Christianity came out of Judaism, yet that doesn't stop us from appreciating our Hebrew heritage. So with our Catholic heritage. We Protestants accepted new truth which reversed the apostasy in Rome, but we still have roots there. The history of the Roman Catholic Church is our history, too, for better or for worse.

Often for the better. Despite the problems in the medieval

church, let's not overlook the good. Monasteries maintained hospitals and provided care for orphans and widows. And all of us owe gratitude to the church for faithfully preserving the Scriptures.

Unfortunately, during the Middle Ages, Bibles were kept chained to monastery walls. The common people had to depend upon secondhand information about the Scriptures. After Erasmus translated the New Testament from Latin, Rome promptly consigned God's Word to its "Index of Prohibited Books." [16]

Without question, the medieval church had forfeited true faith. For a while in the fifteenth century three pontiffs vied for power. Each excommunicated the others, and each labeled the other as antichrist. Thoughtful Christians wondered whether the rival popes were all correct in their estimation of each other.

Of course, times have changed. Since the 1960s with its great "window opening" by Pope John XXIII, many Catholics have been studying the Bible for themselves. No longer do they depend upon the church to tell them what they should believe and do. They find themselves wrestling with the question of church authority in matters such as birth control, enforced celibacy for priests, and similar issues. Catholics today deserve the fervent prayers of other Christians.

Should the church compel the conscience, or is the Bible the only rule of faith? This is the same basic question the Reformers raised in the sixteenth century. Evidently the church has never really resolved the issues of the Reformation.

Certain abuses have been corrected, and the church has adapted itself to our democracy in America. But Rome still rejects the Bible as the only rule of faith. In recent years the German theologian Hans Kung was disciplined after questioning the the pontiff's ability to speak infallibly. Many Catholics worry about the trend away from progress made at Vatican II.

I personally count many Catholics among the dearest Christians I know, and I deeply admire those priests and nuns around the world who faithfully serve in remote mission fields. Many have stood firmly for Christ amid persecution in atheistic societies where some Protestants have compromised their convictions. Our next chapter will explore how churches of the Reformation have largely abandoned their prophetic heritage.

History records that North American Catholics have suffered insult and prejudice. During the 1960 presidential campaign, for example, the Catholic candidate Kennedy faced likely defeat because of religious prejudice. He confronted the issue before a group of Protestant ministers in Houston, where he promised that he would protect the religious rights of all Americans by keeping church and state separate.

Kennedy won the election, of course, and he kept his promise. But today we seem to have forgotten what he realized was so important—safeguarding the boundary between church and state. The United States has gone so far in mixing politics and religion that in 1984 we exchanged ambassadors with the Vatican—with barely a whimper of public protest.

Are we headed over the cliff into a medieval-style union of religion and politics? Will we abolish religious freedom during a military or economic crisis? Is an end-time persecution foretold in Bible prophecy?

Whatever tribulation we will face in the future, thank God we can find safety in the Lord Jesus Christ.

Charles Glass, veteran American journalist, had a nightmare come true when he ventured into South Beirut to investigate a story. Suddenly two cars blocked his path. Before he knew it, terrorists held him captive.

Then followed two months of misery and loneliness, punctuated by moments of terror. But one night Glass heard his guards snoring. This was his time of opportunity! Slipping out the window to a balcony, he made his escape.

About 2:00 a.m. he burst into the lobby of the Summerland Hotel and cried, "I'm Charles Glass. I need a place to hide."

Refuge was granted, and before long he was safely back in the arms of his family.

Friend, as this world prepares for a showdown at Armageddon, we need a place of refuge too. We need the mighty arms of God to shelter us in His care.

Why not open your heart to Him just now and say, "I need a place to hide."

1. "Children's Crusade," in *Grolier's Academic American Encyclopedia,* electronic edition.

2. C. Mervyn Maxwell, *God Cares* (Pacific Press Publishing Association, Boise, Id., 1981) vol. 1, p. 294.

3. "Huguenots" in *Grolier's Academic American Encyclopedia,* electronic edition, estimates a St. Bartholomew's slaughter of between 30,000 and 70,000.

4. Quoted in *S.D.A. Bible Students' Source Book* (Washington, D.C.: Review and Herald Publishing Assn., 1962), pp. 465, 466.

5. LeRoy Froom, *The Prophetic Faith of Our Fathers (Washington, D.C.: Review & Herald, 1954), vol. 2, pp. 528, 784.*

6. Quoted in Maxwell, vol. 1, p. 160. (Emphasis supplied.)

7. Encyclical letter "Chief Duties of Christians," January 10, 1890. Quoted in Maxwell, vol. 1, p. 131.

8. "The Reunion of Christendom," June 20, 1894. Quoted in Maxwell, vol. 1, p. 131.

9. "Torture," *New Catholic Encyclopedia.*

10. "Inquisition," *Ibid.*

11. See Lucius Ferraris, *Prompta Bibliotheca,* 8 vols. (Venice: Caspa Storti, 1772), article "Papa, II." Cited in Maxwell, vol. 1, p. 134.

12. Johann Eck, *Enchiridion of Commonplaces of John Eck Against Luther and Other Enemies of the Church,* trans. F. L. Battles, 2d ed. (Grand Rapids, Mich.: Calvin Theological Seminary, 1978), vol. 8, p. 13. Cited in Maxwell, *God Cares,* vol. 1, p. 134.

13. John A. O'Brien, *The Faith of Millions,* (Huntington, Ind: Our Sunday Visitor, 1974), pp. 400, 401.

14. Froom, vol. 1, p. 713.

15. *Ibid.*

16. Jeremy C. Jackson, *No Other Foundation* (Westchester, Ill.: Cornerstone Books), p. 131: "This major scholarly labor [Erasmus's New Testament] won the unusual honor of being placed first in the list of prohibited books by the Roman church when its 'Index' of forbidden books was introduced."

# Chapter 5

# Antichrist's Civil War

Come with me to the beautiful Tuscany region of north central Italy. As we sail up the Arno River we come to the city of Pisa, a place of fascinating history.

Back in the days of the Roman Empire, Pisa provided a major port for the imperial navy. During medieval times the city rose to economic and political prominence. Today Pisa enjoys fame for its university, its art treasures, and its historical landmarks.

Most notable of Pisa's attractions is the Leaning Tower, which tilts sixteen feet to the side. I've been amazed while visiting there how it keeps from toppling over!

On top of Pisa's leaning bell tower nearly four centuries ago the scientist Galileo is said to have conducted his experiments with gravity. Later he focused his newly made telescope on the heavens, discovering mountains on the moon and spots on the sun. He also learned that the Polish astronomer Copernicus had been correct—the earth revolves like any other planet while the sun remains fixed.

Galileo, the premier scientist of his day, was no stranger to political maneuvering. He named the four satellites of Jupiter which appeared in his telescope after the grand duke of Tuscany, hoping to charm his way onto the grand duke's payroll. It worked. From this seemingly safe base Galileo thought he could promote his new understanding of our solar system. That didn't work out so well.

You see, Copernicus had offended Catholics and Protestants alike with his discoveries. Even Martin Luther protested, "People give ear to an upstart astrologer who strove to show that the *earth* revolves, . . . but sacred Scripture tells us that Joshua commanded the *sun* to stand still, and not the earth." [1] The reformer John Calvin declared, "Who will venture to place the authority of Copernicus above that of the Holy Spirit?" [2]

But Galileo saw no contradiction between science and faith in the Bible. He explained that God in His Word focuses on spiritual truth and usually leaves undisturbed any misconceptions about science. Ancient Joshua imagined that the sun moves across the sky, so thus the Scriptures record it, although in fact the earth revolves around the sun.

Nobody in the seventeenth century could refute Galileo's conclusions, but Christian leaders denounced him as a heretic anyway. Then Pope Urban VIII summoned him before the horrors of the Inquisition.

At stake was Rome's claim to control personal conscience, to be the sole interpreter of the Bible. Since the church had already condemned the Copernican view as "false and opposed to Holy Scripture," Galileo had to disbelieve his telescope or face death.

Galileo recanted rather than be burned at the stake. Even so, the church sentenced the humbled scientist to life imprisonment for "vehement suspicion of heresy." This for the crime of teaching what the whole world believes today.

The year before Galileo was born, Rome set the stage to take action against those who challenged its authority. The church had been suffering enormous losses to the Protestants. By the 1540s all Scandinavia had become Protestant, along with northern Germany, and vast territories throughout Europe. Something had to be done to stop the stampede away from Rome.

The Reformers were demanding that the pope call a church council to discuss their ideas. Many church leaders agreed, though not for the same reason. They wanted Rome to reinforce its authority and unite Catholics in crushing the Reformation. For years Pope Paul III hesitated, but finally in 1545 he called church leaders together in the northern Italian city of Trento.

This Council of Trent continued on and off for years as the debate went back and forth, finally concluding in 1563. It marked a turning point in history, bringing new life to the old church. Much of what we see in Catholicism today came down to us by way of Trent.

The council corrected some of the problems of the past, but refused to reform the church's teachings. Church leaders reaffirmed their beliefs and took the offensive, launching the Counter-Reformation. Through political manipulation, military force, and the Inquisition, Rome regained large territories lost to the Protestants.

The Jesuits were the all-star team of the Counter-Reformation. This new order of clergy trained vigorously for their assignment of turning the tide against the Reformation. Two of their distinguished scholars, Luis de Alcazar and Francisco Ribera, tackled the most serious charge raised by the Protestants: that the church of Rome had become the antichrist.

Alcazar suggested that the prophecies regarding antichrist had been fulfilled in the past with pagan Rome, before the time of the popes. His position became known as *preterism*. Ribera, the father of *futurism*, taught the opposite view. He said that the antichrist would be a *future* enemy of Christianity. Either way, whether the antichrist was past or future, the Jesuits accomplished their purpose. They took the pressure off the pontiff.

How did Ribera manage to put off into the future the prophecies concerning the antichrist? By his artful manipulation of that beautiful prophecy in Daniel 9, the one which foretold the year of Christ's death.[3] Ribera took the heart out of Daniel 9 by replacing Christ with the antichrist. Here's how he did it:

As you will recall from our study in a previous chapter, Daniel foretold that the Messiah would "confirm a covenant" during the seventieth week (the last of the seventy weeks), and "in the middle of the week He shall bring an end to sacrifice and offering." Daniel 9:27. This all happened when Jesus died and the veil of the temple was torn, symbolizing the end of the Old Testament animal sacrifices. But Ribera denied the work of Christ in confirming the covenant. He said the antichrist would fulfill Daniel 9 in the future.

Ribera had no scriptural authority for applying this prophecy to the antichrist. First of all, Daniel 9 obviously involves the saving atonement of Christ on the cross. Second, the One who makes the covenant there confirms it—not breaks it as the futurists claim the antichrist will do. Finally, nowhere in prophecy do we find the antichrist making a covenant with anyone.

Ribera's clever interpretation of Daniel 9 comes down to us today as the "gap theory." You see, he separated the seventieth week there from the rest of the prophecy by a gap of many centuries into the future. But the text in no way calls for such a break or gap between the sixty-ninth and the seventieth week of Daniel 9.

At last Rome had found an answer to the Protestant charge that the church had become the antichrist. No wonder Catholics everywhere rallied around Jesuit scholarship! Ribera's futurism became especially popular. His brilliant disciple Cardinal Robert Bellarmine authored the *Controversies*, a three-volume work opposing the Reformation. Bellarmine gained great fame among Catholics as "the greatest adversary of the Protestant churches."

As we might expect, Protestants rejected Roman Catholic futurism. Of twenty-five prominent Reformation writers between 1639 and the close of the seventeenth century, every one still referred to the antichrist as the papacy. They also maintained their faith that Christ had fulfilled the seventy weeks prophecy of Daniel.

But amazingly—incredibly—Protestants in the last two centuries have abandoned the prophetic faith of the Reformers by adopting the futurism of the Jesuits! Of all the astonishing developments in church history, nothing surpasses this. George Eldon Ladd, a respected scholar of our time, documents it in his book *The Blessed Hope*:

It will probably come as a shock to many modern futurists to be told that the first scholar in relatively modern times who returned to the patristic futuristic interpretation was a Spanish Jesuit named Ribera. In 1590, Ribera published a commentary on the Revelation as a counter-interpretation to the prevailing view among Protestants which identified the Papacy with the antichrist. Ribera applied all of Revelation but the earliest chapters to the end time rather than to the history of the Church. Antichrist would be a single evil person who would be received by the Jews and would rebuild Jerusalem, abolish Christianity, deny Christ, persecute the Church and rule the world for three and a half years.[4]

No doubt about it, the Protestant world has suffered a serious loss of its prophetic faith. How did this apostasy happen?

It began in the early nineteenth century over in the British Isles. Edward Irving, a minister of the Church of Scotland, became interested in Christ's second coming and cofounded the Society for the Investigation of Prophecy. Unfortunately, he accepted Ribera's futurism and even translated a book written by a Spanish Jesuit missionary. Irving preached with great success. He captivated interest in London's high society and once addressed an outdoor audience of 12,000 in Scotland.

One Sunday morning in 1831 a woman speaking in tongues interrupted Irving's sermon. Unusual experiments with faith healing followed. Irving, being open-minded, hoped all this might be the work of the Holy Spirit. He became further involved in questionable doctrine before disaffected members accused him of heresy and voted him out of his pulpit.

Edward Irving died brokenhearted in his early forties. Yet his influence lived on. Through Irving, the Irish Anglican John Nelson Darby adopted Ribera's futurism. This earnest young man began traveling around Europe and crossed the Atlantic to the United States, spreading his beliefs everywhere he went. By his death in 1882 Darby could count nearly 100 study groups in America alone dedicated to his ideas.

After Darby died, the torch of futurism passed to C. I. Scofield, compiler of the study notes in the Scofield Reference Bible. First published in 1909, Scofield's Bible remains enormously popular today. And since 1970 Hal Lindsey's best-seller *The Late Great Planet Earth* has persuaded millions of Protestants to believe futurist teaching about the antichrist.

Think of it—an actual diversionary teaching of the church of Rome unthinkingly accepted with open arms by the Protestant world! With all this confusion about Bible prophecy, have we been set up for an unexpected encounter with the antichrist at Armageddon?

Well, we can appreciate the renewed interest today in Bible prophecy and the second coming of Jesus. But anyone who understands the Reformation must feel concerned that Protestants have lost their prophetic heritage. Shouldn't we still be riding on the shoulders of the Reformers?

The Catholic Counter-Reformation gained more ground than Francisco Ribera could have dreamed possible. No longer did the church need to fight the Reformers' charge that the papacy was the antichrist. Rome rests secure now that conservative Protestants are teaching Catholic futurism!

What an incredible turn of events, wouldn't you say? Are we not in a dangerous position now, vulnerable to false theories about the antichrist?

Some would ask, "What difference does it make, so long as we are sincere Christians?" But if we are *truly* sincere, we will take Bible prophecy seriously when it warns about deception, don't you think?

Back in Christ's day, you recall, ignorance of Bible prophecy led many to reject Him. They expected a Messiah who would drive out the occupying Roman army, and when Jesus merely healed the sick and raised the dead, they didn't think He qualified! Even faithful John the Baptist became confused. He sent a couple of messengers to Jesus with the question, "Are You the Coming One, or do we look for another?" Matthew 11:3.

Such doubts and delusions troubled the whole nation. The controversy climaxed during the closing months of Christ's life. In John 7 we find Jesus in Jerusalem attending the Feast of Tabernacles. During that annual fall festival "there was much murmuring among the people concerning Him. Some said, 'He is good'; others said, 'No, on the contrary, He deceives the people.' " John 7:12.

The debate about Jesus raged back and forth. Once again a popular misconception of Bible prophecy led Christ's hearers to doubt His identity. They whispered, "We know where this Man is from; but when the Christ comes, no one knows where He is from." Verse 27.

You see, many believed that the Messiah would appear suddenly and mysteriously out of nowhere. As for Jesus, He had been around for a while and therefore couldn't be the one. Or so they thought. Their complete ignorance of prophecy caused them to spurn their Saviour.

Others knew a little more about the Scriptures but still rejected Jesus. They realized that the Messiah would be born in the little town of Bethlehem, as Jesus indeed was—but His background in Galilee troubled them. Raising their eyebrows they inquired, " 'Will the Christ come out of Galilee? Has not the Scripture said that the Christ comes from the seed of David and from the town of Bethlehem, where David was?' So there was a division among the people because of Him." John 7:41-43.

A little investigation would have solved their perplexity. The Scriptures had predicted long ago that Messiah would live in Nazareth after He was born in Bethlehem. See Matthew 2:23. But false information about prophecy led Israel to reject Jesus.

So you see, misinformation about prophecy can prove even worse than no information at all. People think they know, when they are sadly mistaken.

Many in Christ's day didn't bother studying the Bible for themselves. What mattered to them was, "Have any of the rulers or the Pharisees believed on Him?" John 7:48. In other words, "Does anybody famous believe? I'm not going to follow truth until some important religious teacher leads the way."

Do we still hear people saying the same today?

You know the sad story back then. Jesus failed Israel's expectations, so they failed to accept Him—all because of their unwillingness to investigate the prophecies with an open and willing heart.

Do we stand in similar danger today? Remember Paul's warning about the antichrist: "Let no one deceive you by any means." 2 Thessalonians 2:3. Are we being urged to scout the horizon for some future antichrist power, when all the time it has been flourishing in our own back yard?

Something to think about carefully.

Remember that God's people didn't recognize Christ when He came because they expected a different kind of Messiah than Bible prophecy had actually predicted. Perhaps in our day we won't identify the antichrist because of similar confusion about prophecy. Will some unknowing Christians even cooperate with the antichrist in his deceptions? What a setting this would be for Armageddon!

We had better be careful, wouldn't you say? There's too much at stake in this crisis hour to be careless—or to take someone else's word. God help us study the Bible for ourselves and then follow its sure word of prophecy.

---

1. Quoted in B. Russell, *A History of Western Philosophy* (New York: Simon & Schuster, 1945), p. 528. Cited by Wallbank et al,

*Civilization Past and Present* (Glenview, Ill: Scott, Foresman & Co., 1969), p. 554. (Emphasis supplied.)

2. *Ibid.*, p. 528.

3. Please refer to our discussion of Daniel 9 in chapter 2 of this book.

4. George Eldon Ladd, *The Blessed Hope* (Grand Rapids, Mich.: Eerdmans Publishing Co., 1956), pp. 37, 38.

# Chapter 6

# Secret of the Rapture

"There I was, driving down the freeway and all of a sudden the place went crazy . . . cars going in all directions . . . and not one of them had a driver. I mean it was wild! I think we've got an invasion from outer space!"

What do we have here—a dream? A nightmare? Or maybe even a religious fiction thriller? This vivid scene comes from *The Late Great Planet Earth*,[1] Hal Lindsey's book about the "rapture" and earth's final crisis.

The rapture, explains Lindsey, is the sudden, silent, and invisible coming of Jesus to snatch the saints away from this world. Then follow seven years inside heaven's pearly gates, after which Jesus will return here to overcome the antichrist in a showdown at the Battle of Armageddon.

Quite an intriguing scenario! No wonder Christians everywhere have become excited about it. You've seen the bumper stickers: "Warning: Driver Will Be Raptured Any Moment." Or, "If I'm Raptured Take the Wheel."

It will happen very soon, rapturists believe. They point to the establishment of Israel as a nation back in 1948 and recall what Jesus said, "This generation will by no means pass away till all these things are fulfilled." Matthew 24:34. Rapturists have figured that a generation equals forty years or so. Therefore the end should come around 1988.

But wait. The secret rapture is already long overdue. It should have happened around 1981, launching seven years of tribulation on earth. After that, Christ was supposed to return with His saints in 1988. This is what many rapturists were teaching in the 1970s.

Well, you can imagine how millions of them felt when Christ failed to take them up to heaven back then. The *Chicago Sun Times* reported how fifty members of the Lighthouse Gospel Foundation of Tucson quit their jobs and disposed of property in anticipation of the rapture on June 28, 1981. One of their members, a young physician, testified, "I've never known such peace, such joy."

I wonder how he felt after his prophetic expectations failed.

Even now Christ has not yet returned for His people, so the rapture has had to be rescheduled. But it still *will* happen any time, we are told. Any moment Jesus will come and sneak His people away.

Many Christians believe this with all their hearts. Many other Christians feel that rapturists are seriously mistaken. How can we know the truth? We had better go to our Bibles.

First we find that the word *rapture* itself is not in the English Bible. It comes from a Latin word meaning "to carry away," which applied in the commonly accepted religious sense means to be carried away when the Lord comes. The word translated *rapture* shows up in the Latin version of 1 Thessalonians 4:16, 17:

"The Lord Himself will descend from heaven with a shout, with the voice of an archangel, and with the trumpet of God. And the dead in Christ will rise first. Then we who are alive and remain shall be caught up together [raptured] with them in the clouds to meet the Lord in the air. And thus we shall always be with the Lord."

Imagine how wonderful it will be to hear Jesus shout for joy as He descends from heaven to take us home. And to listen to the mighty blast from the trumpet of God. Christ's coming for His people will be the most vocal, the most spectacular event of all time.

Well, with all this shouting and trumpeting, you wonder

how secret the rapture will really be! Maybe it won't be secret at all.

Evidently not. And come to think of it, why would Jesus have to sneak us up to heaven? How much more appropriate for our coming King to burst triumphantly through the clouds and call us home. That's what the Bible teaches.

Many rapturists are surprised to discover that the Bible never says Christ will come in the twinkling of an eye. It says when Jesus comes *"we shall all be changed—in a moment, in the twinkling of an eye,* at the last trumpet. For the trumpet will sound, and the dead will be raised incorruptible, and we shall be changed." 1 Corinthians 15:51, 52.

You see, the change of our bodies from mortal to eternal will happen instantly—but Christ's coming itself will be loud enough and long enough for trumpets to sound. Notice the words of Jesus Himself:

"Then the sign of the Son of Man will appear in heaven, and then all the tribes of the earth will mourn, and they will *see* the Son of Man coming on the clouds of heaven with power and great glory. And He will send His angels with a great sound of a trumpet, and they will gather together His elect." Matthew 24:30, 31.

Everyone on earth, saved or lost, will know it when Jesus returns to gather His elect saints. Now, the Bible does say that Christ will come unexpectedly like a thief in the night. But does that mean the world will not realize when it is happening?

Remember Pearl Harbor on that fateful morning of December 7, 1941. Even though American intelligence had warned of an imminent attack, the Japanese caught us unaware. Their attack was a closely guarded secret, but when those bombers dove out of the sky, everyone knew what was happening.

So it will be at the return of Jesus. Despite worldwide warnings, the unsaved will be caught by surprise—but they will certainly be aware of Christ's presence.

What will happen to those who are not ready to meet Jesus? Will they have further opportunity to repent? That's what secret rapturists teach. Oh, they will have to survive some pretty severe tribulation, but they can still be saved.

Here we must pause to ask a disturbing question: What if this second chance idea is false—what if human probation ends at Christ's coming? Let's see what the Bible tells us:

"As it was in the days of Noah, so it will be also in the days of the Son of Man: They ate, they drank, they married wives, they were given in marriage, until the day that Noah entered the ark, and the flood came and destroyed them all." Luke 17:26, 27.

You know how it was in the days of Noah: business as usual until that fatal surprise came from the sky. All who had neglected God's warning lost their lives. "Even so will it be in the day when the Son of Man is revealed." Luke 17:30.

After Christ's coming, dead bodies will be scattered across the earth. Yes, Jesus said some would be taken and some would be left—but those left behind are left dead:

" 'Two people will be in one bed; one will be taken and the other left. Two women will be grinding grain together; one will be taken and the other left.' 'Where Lord?' they asked. He replied 'Where there is a dead body, there the vultures will gather.' " Luke 17:34-37, NIV. So everyone who is ready to meet Jesus He will take up to heaven. Anyone who is unprepared will remain here dead—and tragically, left on the ground for vultures to consume. No second chance! Are you beginning to see the danger in this secret rapture teaching? If our unsaved friends and relatives don't make their decision before Christ comes, they can never be saved. As God's Word puts it, "Behold, now is the day of salvation!" 2 Corinthians 6:2.

So you see, the secret rapture simply isn't scriptural. It's a medieval myth—a carryover from the sixteenth century Counter-Reformation, which we studied in our last chapter.

Protestant scholars during Reformation times all believed

that Christ's coming for His people would be anything but secret. An Old Testament prophecy in the book of Daniel convinced them of it. Let's look at the evidence in Daniel 2. We find a dream here which God gave to an ancient monarch. Watch the fascinating drama as it unfolds.

The king: Nebuchadnezzar of Babylon. The time: 600 years before Christ. The hero of the hour: Daniel again, that teenage captive from Judah now promoted to the royal court.

God wanted to get the attention of the proud ruler, so He gave Nebuchadnezzar that dream one night—only to cause him to forget its message when morning dawned. The king remembered only that whatever he had dreamed was quite spectacular and significant.

Desperately, Nebuchadnezzar demanded that his psychic counselors tell him the dream which he forgot and its interpretation. They were supposed to know. But when they didn't, he condemned them all to die. And because the king didn't understand the difference between a psychic and a prophet, Daniel was rounded up with the others to be executed.

His life at stake, Daniel asked for an audience with the king. He requested time to pray to his God, promising to return with both the dream and its meaning. The king agreed.

And did God fail Daniel? Not in the least. In a night vision He revealed to His young prophet what the king had dreamed and what it meant.

The next morning Daniel quickly headed for the palace, where the king was waiting eagerly. Could this unpretentious young captive possibly do what his trusted counselors could not? We pick up the story in Daniel 2:31. Listen with the king as Daniel recounts what he had dreamed:

"You, O king, were watching; and behold, a great image! This great image, whose splendor was excellent, stood before you; and its form was awesome."

Intently the king watches the noble face of God's youthful messenger as he continues: "This image's head was of fine gold, its chest and arms of silver, its belly and thighs of bronze, its legs of iron, its feet partly of iron and partly of clay." Verses 32, 33.

Absolutely spellbound, Nebuchadnezzar, proud monarch of the mighty Babylonian empire, stares at Daniel in amazement. This humble servant of heaven's God is reporting with uncanny accuracy the dream which had escaped his memory.

Daniel goes on: "You watched while a stone was cut out without hands, which struck the image on its feet of iron and clay, and broke them in pieces. Then the iron, the clay, the bronze, the silver, and the gold were crushed together, and became like chaff from the summer threshing floors; the wind carried them away so that no trace of them was found. And the stone that struck the image became a great mountain and filled the whole earth." Verses 34, 35.

The king relived the startling scene. He saw again the majestic image with the head of glittering gold, its breast and arms of polished silver. He saw again the body and thighs of burnished brass, the legs of solid iron, and strangest of all, the mixture of iron and clay from which the feet were formed. But why was the gold replaced by silver, and the silver by brass? What was the meaning of the huge stone which knocked the statue down? Would Daniel tell him?

Leaning to the edge of his throne, the monarch waited breathlessly as Daniel prepared to interpret. And now the moment he had been waiting for: "You, O king, are . . . this head of gold." Verses 37, 38.

"How flattering!" Nebuchadnezzar imagined. How fitting that his kingdom should be represented by the head of gold. After all, were not historians already calling Babylon the "golden kingdom"?

But then followed some bad news for Babylon. Nebuchadnezzar raised his royal eyebrows as Daniel continued: "But after you shall arise another kingdom inferior to yours." Verse 39.

What? His kingdom to come to an end? Babylon to be succeeded, and by an inferior power at that!

Yes, Babylon would not last forever. It was only the first of a series of kingdoms which would succeed upon the ruins of one another. Cyrus the Persian would conquer Babylon even in Daniel's day. It happened during the feast of Belshazzar—remember the handwriting on the wall?

The double monarchy of the Medes and the Persians, represented by the two silver arms of the statue, ruled for two centuries. Today it also lies in ruins, for prophecy had decreed that "another, a third kingdom of bronze, . . . shall rule over all the earth." Verse 39.

This bronze kingdom was Greece, led by Alexander the Great. This ambitious leader climaxed his lightning conquests in the battle of Arbela, 331 years before Christ. At the incredibly youthful age of twenty-five he reigned as master of all he surveyed—but seven years later he was dead. So swiftly does earthly glory fade.

Now came the fourth kingdom of iron, which has to be Rome, the iron monarchy of history. In the days of that empire Jesus lived and died. Roman soldiers officiated at the crucifixion, and a Roman seal closed His tomb.

Four world empires. And would you not expect that if there were four, there might also be a fifth, arising upon the ruins of the fourth?

But no. The divine forecast states in verse 41: "Whereas you saw the feet and toes, partly of potter's clay and partly of iron, the kingdom shall be divided."

Something new here. A change would take place, a division. And did it happen? Yes. During the fourth and fifth centuries several distinct nations emerged within the boundaries of Western Rome. The mighty empire of the Caesars disintegrated before the onslaughts of barbarians, and in her place we see the well-known nations of Germany, France, Switzerland, Portugal, England, Spain, and Italy.

I ask you, could human wisdom predict the future with such accuracy? No. Fulfilled Bible prophecy stamps the Word of God as divine. But now we come to verse 43. This is what we have been waiting for: "As you saw iron mixed with ceramic clay, they will mingle with the seed of men; but they will not adhere to one another, just as iron does not mix with clay."

What do you think of that? Seven words that doom world conquest: "They will not adhere to one another." Europe will never stick together under one government, according to the sure word of prophecy.

We notice an interesting pattern in world history. Nebuchadnezzar had no difficulty ruling the world, nor did Cyrus or Alexander or the Caesars. But then everything changed. Since the days of the Roman Empire, history has been like a broken record. It tells the story of every would-be dictator in one persistent word: "Defeat, defeat, defeat!"

That one word tells the story of Charlemagne, Louis XIV, Napoleon, Kaiser Wilhelm, Hitler, and every dreaming dictator who yet may follow. And back of it all is a power-packed prophecy.

Napoleon had seemed the superman of destiny. In 1799 he seized France and set out to unite the remaining segments of the empire in Europe. But you remember how God used the Duke of Wellington to dramatically fulfill Daniel 2 at Waterloo, when Napoleon's idea of world empire collapsed.

A century passed. Then Kaiser Wilhelm set out with the same idea in 1914, and we all know the end of that story. Even while news of fresh disaster poured in from every front, a corporal in action on the crumbling German lines entered a hospital. Nothing much seemed to be wrong with him, but he appeared so completely devastated that the hospital assigned him a cot.

Then this defiant soldier turned his face to the wall and refused to acknowledge the defeat of Germany. Two days later Adolf Hitler rose from that bed and left the hospital with a feverish desire to marshal the world under his banner. And that story, too, has been written in ashes with the blood and the tears of millions.

Hitler was doomed to failure by God's Word in Daniel 2.

He who knows the end from the beginning says that the broken pieces of the Roman Empire will never cleave together. Time and agan, military leaders and peace agencies alike have tried and failed through those simple words, "They will not adhere to one another." Any attempt to unite Europe is bound to come to naught.

And now the climax of it all, the destiny of the nations—your destiny and mine—is found in the words of Daniel 2:44: "In the days of these kings the God of heaven will set up a kingdom which shall never be destroyed; and the kingdom shall not be left to other people; it shall break in pieces and consume all these kingdoms, and it shall stand forever."

Not in the days of Babylon or Persia or Greece or Rome, but down in the days of those kings—in our time—God will set up His kingdom.

And notice that Christ's coming kingdom will shatter all other kingdoms on this planet. Life will end on earth with no second chance for repentance. And it won't be a secret rapture—this grand climax of the ages will be seen and heard by all.

Wonderful news indeed! This is not sensationalism, not wild or fanciful speculation about prophecy. Daniel 2 brings us the certain message from God's Word that the next great event of history will be the coming of our Lord Jesus Christ in power and glory.

Friend, have you placed yourself on God's side? Now is the time to do so. Now is the day of salvation.

The King is coming! If His coming does not fit into your plans, then by all means change your plans. God will help you.

---

1. Hal Lindsey, *The Late Great Planet Earth* (New York: Bantam Books, 1979) pp. 124, 125.

# Chapter 7

# Planet Earth's New Age

A strange sound welcomed the dawning day on Mount Shasta. The eerie chant dipped and rose over the chilly slopes as forty young Californians stretched their arms toward the rising sun. Then, holding hands around a circle, they began humming, along with 5,000 other celebrants on the mountain.

Unusual happenings are nothing new out here in California, but this was more than typical summer madness. "Harmonic convergence," they called it. All over the world that Sunday, "New Age" believers gathered in thirty-six spots they consider sacred. In places like the Grand Canyon, the Pyramids of Egypt, and on Mount Fuji in Japan, they met to welcome a New Age of peace and love.

For months New Age devotees had been studying ancient prophecies of the North American Indians, linking them with the sun worship calendars of South American Maya and Aztec Indians. They concluded that a special alignment of planets and constellations on Sunday and Monday, August 16 and 17 of 1987, would produce cleansing energy for our planet.

New Age believers saw a unique opportunity—this was supposedly the first time in 23,412 years that the heavens had poised themselves in such a blessed position. Emile Canning, the group leader on Mount Shasta, implored, "144,000 sun dancers filled with the sun will bring on the New Age. Allow yourself to become one of the 144,000, one of the dancing suns." World peace and relief from catastrophe would result.

They got their numbers that Sunday—more than the required 144,000 sun dancers. But their hopes for a New Age failed them. That very night Northwest Flight 255 crashed in Detroit, the second-worst single air disaster in the history of the United States. Hardly what New Age believers expected from their incantations.

The weekend also passed without the massive UFO sightings some had predicted. Probably the closest thing to an alien visit was reported by one of Shasta's residents: "We're seeing a form on our television that looks something like a dove with two widespread wings—we can't explain it."

Well, perhaps a TV repairman could.

Or maybe not. Something more than the ridiculous was happening. The New Age movement had joined hands with the spirit world. Events of the weekend included "channeling," where famous departed personalities supposedly disclosed their harmonic wishes through psychic mediums. In a meadow beneath Shasta's fir-covered slopes, 200 pilgrims from Los Angeles paid $35 each to listen reverently as John the Apostle (from Bible times, you know) spoke to them through channeler Jerry Bowman. So they imagined.

Enough of this unbiblical speculation now, wouldn't you say? It won't cost us $35 to discover what the apostle John really said about the new age. In his New Testament Gospel he quoted the words of Jesus: "In My Father's house are many mansions; . . . I go to prepare a place for you." Then He promised, "I will come again and receive you to Myself; that where I am, there you may be also." John 14:2, 3.

What a wonderful eternity we will have in the Lord Jesus Christ! This new age, as the Bible explains, begins with Christ's coming in power and glory. Picture the glorious scene: The Son of God piercing the vaulted heavens, moving down the star-studded highway of the skies, attended by myriads of angels. Then He calls out with a voice of thunder, "Awake, you that sleep in the dust of the earth! Arise to everlasting life!"

And loved ones you have lost will hear. That voice calling the dead will be heard the world around. Families will be united. Children snatched away by death will be placed again in their parents' arms. What a reunion day!

As the resurrected saints are drawn upward to meet Jesus, we who have been living join them in the air. Imagine the feeling! Defying gravity, we soar through the sky. Without a spacesuit we sail through the stars up to our heavenly home.

And when we get there, what a welcome will await us. Angels crowding about us, singing songs of praise to God. We will sit down to a homecoming banquet better than any dinner ever enjoyed on earth. And best of all, the heavenly Father Himself will introduce us to our paradise home.

What a home it will be! Mansions—what will they be like? Certainly more glorious than the richest dwellings on earth. I can hardly wait to see them, can you? Even more, I can hardly wait to see the Lord Himself, our heavenly King!

What will we do after we settle into our new celestial home? The book of Revelation unfolds more of God's plan: "Blessed and holy is he who has part in the first resurrection. Over such the second death has no power, but they shall be priests of God and of Christ, and shall reign with Him a thousand years." Revelation 20:6.

The raising of believers when Christ comes is called the first resurrection. Will there be a resurrection for unbelievers as well? Yes. Verse 5 of Revelation 20 tells about it: "The rest of the dead did not live again until the thousand years were finished."

So a second resurrection at the end of a thousand years will raise up those who rejected Jesus. They will face judgment and second death, as we will see later in this chapter.

We may wonder, "Why does God wait a thousand years to dispense with sin?" Simply this. He will not destroy the wicked until all the universe fully understands why—until you and I understand. That is why Paul speaks of a time when "the saints will judge the world." 1 Corinthians 6:2. This will be during our thousand years in heaven, according to Revelation 20:4.

God will open the books to us, and there will be plenty of time to get our questions answered. Questions about things we never understood, such as, Why did God let Baby Jenny die? And why didn't He heal Aunt Ellen with all her faith?

You know, often this side of eternity, life appears to be just a tangled mess—when all the time God was working for our good. He will explain it all to us in heaven. Now we "see in a mirror, dimly" (1 Corinthians 13:12), but then we will finally understand what we can now accept only by faith.

Our vital questions will be answered. Curious questions too. Jesus said that there is nothing covered on earth that will not be revealed. See Luke 12:2. There is nothing hidden now that will not be known then.

How fascinating it will be to learn the secrets of history. Secrets of the Kremlin and the White House and the Mafia. Secrets of the pharaohs and the caesars and the popes.

When we get to heaven and look around, new questions will confront us. Questions like, Where is my pastor? Why didn't he make it—I thought he was such a godly man! Some we imagined were saved will be missing up there, and others we thought were lost will be saved. As Jesus predicted, many of the first will be last and the last first.

God will take the time to explain it all. We will see that He has indeed done everything possible to save every soul throughout human history. When all our questions have been answered in heaven, we will be prepared to witness the solemn punishment of the unsaved at the end of the thousand years.

During our time up in heaven, what will be happening down on earth? According to Hal Lindsey's *The Late Great Planet Earth*, the rapture of the saints begins a "seven-year countdown" before a showdown at Armageddon. Here are Lindsey's own words: "After the Christians are gone [raptured] God is going to reveal Himself in a special way . . . to 144,000 Jewish Billy Grahams turned loose on this earth—

the earth will never know a period of evangelism like this period. These Jewish people are going to make up for lost time. They are going to have the greatest number of converts in all history." [1]

So rapturists believe that after Christ comes, the Jewish people will finally accept Him and lead countless others to salvation. While all these Jews are being converted (according to the scenario anticipated by the rapture theory), the forces of evil will be accelerating their efforts to undermine the progress of the gospel. The antichrist, a Roman dictator, rises to power out of the ten-nation confederacy of the European Common Market. He signs a protection treaty with the nation of Israel, which enables the Israelis to rebuild the Jerusalem temple in three and a half years. So says Lindsey.

Rapturists believe the temple will scarcely be rebuilt when the antichrist will break his covenant with the Jews and disrupt the temple services. Then will follow three and a half additional years of terrible tribulation during antichrist's cruel reign, which Lindsey claims "will make the regimes of Hitler, Mao, and Stalin look like Girl Scouts weaving a daisy chain by comparison." [2]

A colossal military struggle will bring on Armageddon. At that climactic moment, Christ will return once again to earth with the church (those who were raptured seven years earlier) to destroy the antichrist and all ungodly forces. He will then rule the world from Jerusalem.

Quite an impressive theory. But how much of it is factual? How much of it is scriptural?

Let's remember what the apostle Paul taught about the antichrist. He said this deceptive power would bring tribulation to God's people *before* the rapture. See 2 Thessalonians 2:3.

Every one of the Reformers realized that antichrist and the tribulation would come before Christ's second coming. Not until the Counter-Reformation undermined their prophetic faith did Protestants believe otherwise.

If you recall, we discovered in our last chapter that the unsaved will be struck dead when Jesus comes to take the saved to heaven. See Luke 17:26-37. Their bodies will be scattered over the earth.

Do you realize that one day soon, within the space of a few short hours, this earth will be depopulated—not one human being left alive anywhere in the world? We hear the gloomy predictions about how this world would look after a nuclear war—a dismal gray wasteland. An Old Testament prophecy describing our planet after Jesus comes bears striking resemblance to the eerie scene scientists warn us about:

"I beheld the earth, and indeed it was without form, and void; and the heavens, they had no light. I beheld the mountains, and indeed they trembled, and all the hills moved back and forth. I beheld, and indeed there was no man, and all the birds of the heavens had fled. I beheld, and indeed the fruitful land was a wilderness, and all its cities were broken down at the presence of the Lord, by His fierce anger. For thus says the Lord: 'The whole land shall be desolate; yet I will not make a full end.' " Jeremiah 4:23-27.

The prophet describes the earth after Christ comes as being without form and void—just like in the first chapter of Genesis, before creation was complete. No human life remains; even the birds have fled. You see, sinners won't have a second chance. When Christ returns, all will have had their last opportunity.

Is this morbid scene the final chapter of earth's history? No! Did you notice the ray of hope? God promises, "Yet I will not make a full end." Evidently He still has plans for this planet, as we will see shortly.

Where will Satan spend the thousand years of earth's emptiness? Revelation 20 explains that the devil will be exiled, confined to this earth in a "bottomless pit" with no one to tempt. See Revelation 20:1-3.

Now, you can't lock up Satan with a literal key or restrain him with a real chain, and no bottomless pit, no yawning chasm, could hold him. So what could this mean? It's simply a symbolic way of saying that Satan will at last be stopped. He and his angels will be confined to this earth.

Today Satan roams as a roaring lion, looking for people to devour with temptation. But after Jesus comes every human being will be either dead or gone. The great rebel will have nothing to do for a thousand years, except to wander over the dark and desolate earth amid the ruin he caused.

But the Bible says that the devil will be loosed again after being retired for 1,000 years. Evidently he will have his wicked followers back, as we read here: "Now when the thousand years have expired, Satan will be released from his prison and will go out to deceive the nations which are in the four corners of the earth, Gog and Magog, to gather them together to battle, whose number is as the sand of the sea." Verses 7, 8.

Now things happen quite quickly. Satan, loosed by the resurrection of the lost, assumes leadership of his newly resurrected host of rebels. What happens next? The drama unfolds in verse 9:

"They went up on the breadth of the earth and surrounded the camp of the saints and the beloved city. And fire came down from God out of heaven and devoured them."

What a scenario! How did the Holy City, the camp of the saints, get down here? Were we not up in heaven with Jesus? This is so incredible that I couldn't believe it myself if I didn't see it in the Bible. Revelation 21:1-3 says:

"I saw a new heaven and a new earth, for the first heaven and the first earth had passed away. Also there was no more sea. Then I, John, saw the holy city, New Jerusalem, coming down out of heaven from God, prepared as a bride adorned for her husband. And I heard a loud voice from heaven saying, 'Behold, the tabernacle of God is with men, and He will dwell with them, and they shall be His people, and God Himself will be with them and be their God.'"

Can you imagine what it will be like for us to travel from heaven back to earth and watch the Holy City descend from heaven? According to the Old Testament prophet Zechariah,

Christ will stand that day upon the Mount of Olives, just outside the ruins of present Jerusalem. His feet will divide the mountain into a great plain on which the New Jerusalem will rest. See Zechariah 14:3, 4.

You know the beatitude, "Blessed are the poor in spirit, for theirs is the kingdom of heaven." But Jesus also promised, "Blessed are the meek, for they shall inherit the earth." Not this poisoned old planet that we know now, but a new earth, pure and unpolluted, redeemed from the ravages of sin, following our thousand years in heaven.

After the Holy City has settled on this earth, everyone who has ever lived will be alive together inside or outside the city. Picture the scene. Satan compares his vast host with the much smaller number within the city. Numbers favor his side, and he has the greatest military leaders of history supporting him. Hitler is there, along with bold and skilled generals who never lost a battle. Satan rallies his forces for a final, frenzied attack against God's throne and the Holy City. The vast army of rebels advances.

Then what happens? Hell happens. "Fire came down from God out of heaven and devoured them." The earth becomes a vast, seething lake of fire. But the city of God rides safely upon it, just as Noah's ark rode safely upon the waters of the flood.

Hell will be hot—so hot that sin and sinners won't survive. But after those flames have done their work, they will go out. Just as the water receded in Noah's day and the ark settled back down on the earth, so the lake of fire will subside and the Holy City will rest secure on a purified planet. God will bring beauty out of ashes, re-creating the earth as beautifully as the long-lost Eden.

I wish we had more space in this chapter to discuss your questions about hell. If you want more information, just write for my book *Impersonation Game*.[3] It will be my gift to you.

Well, finally the rebellion will be over, never to trouble a happy universe again. Sin will be gone, and with it death and pain and heartache. God will give this born-again planet to

His people as their permanent paradise home.

Why would God move the capital city of the universe from heaven down to our lowly planet? Because we are His special people. God so loved the world that He gave His beloved Son to us. Jesus was not a loan, but a gift, and He still belongs to us today. Forever, our Saviour will be one of the human family, our Brother as well as our Lord!

And Jerusalem, where Jesus suffered and died for our sins, will be the place of God's eternal throne. Throughout ceaseless ages, the citizens of the universe will worship with us at the site of our salvation.

I want to be there, don't you!

Whether or not you realize it, this moment you are deciding your eternal destiny. When the fire falls, you don't have to be locked outside the Holy City with the devil and the doomed. You can be safely inside with the Lord Jesus Christ!

Just now, why not surrender your life to His will. Place your trust in His salvation, and you will be included in God's new age on planet earth.

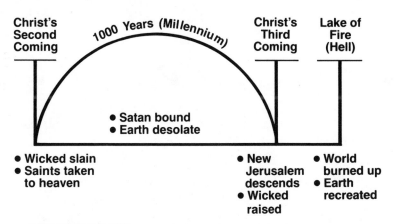

1. Lindsey, *Planet Earth*, pp. 99, 100.

2. *Ibid.*, p. 99.

3. Write to: It Is Written, P. O. Box 1000, Thousand Oaks, CA 91360.

# Chapter 8

# Counterfeiting Armageddon

Armageddon! The word sends shivers up our spines, just the mention of it sparks all kinds of fearful speculation. Does anybody really know what will happen during the showdown at Armageddon? World War III, perhaps?

A week or so after Inauguration Day in 1977, President Carter's assistant for national security decided to run a test. He had been briefed on plans for helping the President escape in the event of an attack on Washington. So Brzezinski went to the officer in charge. With a smile he asked if he really could get the President out before the missiles came in.

"Yes, Sir," the man answered. "That's why I'm here."

"Have you practiced?" Brzezinski wanted to know.

"Of course," the officer proudly assured him. "We test this system all the time."

"That's good, because the President authorized me to do just that." Brzezinski then pushed back his left sleeve and pressed a button on his watch. "Pretend I'm the President. Pretend an alarm has sounded. Get me to safety."

"Now?" the officer stammered.

"*Now!*" Brzezinski pushed the button again, and the seconds began to fly.

The officer protested. "You can't mean now. It's dark. It's snowing. It's—"

He was cut short by a look that stunned him. He babbled a series of breathless orders into the phone.

Brzezinski then dashed for the back lawn of the White House to meet the rescue helicopter. On the way outside he grabbed a secretary to play the role of the first lady.

The helicopter should have been ready to go, but three precious minutes went by as they waited. Five minutes. Finally it dropped down to take them away.

Airborne at last, Brzezinski began testing communications. "Call the joint chiefs," he ordered. And the crewman put the call through the White House switchboard.

"Don't bother to continue. If this were really an attack, that switchboard would be demolished by now."

So it went. It took twice the allotted time to reach the big jet which would whisk the President away to safety. Known as the doomsday plane, this elaborately modified 747 stands by on constant alert, ready to take off in three minutes. It wasn't.

One thing more. This little test could easily have been Mr. Brzezinski's last flight. For the officer in charge was so nervous and confused he forgot to alert the Secret Service guards. They almost shot down the escape helicopter as an intruder.

The newspaper article from which I took this story was entitled, "Cruising to Armageddon."

Whatever Armageddon really is, it seems like we aren't quite ready for it. Even so, we are obsessed with knowing all we can about earth's ultimate crisis. Only such curiosity can explain the extraordinary sales of *The Late Great Planet Earth*.

Let's examine the blueprint for Armageddon proposed by author Hal Lindsey. He envisions a dramatic sequence of events involving conspiracy, double-dealing, and all-out war among world powers.

It all begins three and a half years after the "rapture," when the antichrist is supposed to break his covenant with the Jews. He disrupts the temple services in Jerusalem and stops the animal sacrifices (which, we are told, will have been reinstated). Lindsey calls this the "abomination of desolation" that triggers the great tribulation and sets the stage for Armageddon.

The next step toward doomsday happens when an Arab-African army attacks Israel. Suddenly the Soviets double-cross their Arab allies and launch their own invasion of the Middle East. According to Lindsey's scenario, the Russians will succeed in gaining control over the entire area.

Now the plot really thickens. The antichrist quickly marshals a vast army from the European Common Market confederacy and Red China, with perhaps the United States joining in. This huge host enables the antichrist to demolish the Soviet occupation of Israel.

Lindsey says the complete annihilation of Arab-African and Soviet armies will leave only two great powers to wrestle for world dominion: "the combined forces of the Western civilization united under the leadership of the Roman Dictator [the antichrist] and the vast hordes of the Orient probably united under the Red Chinese war machine." [1]

Finally, according to Lindsey's prediction, these two remaining powers will fight for control of the world. The battlefield will be the plain of Megiddo in northern Israel. At the climax of this Armageddon war Christ will return with His saints to destroy all the ungodly and set up His kingdom in Jerusalem to rule the world.

Breathtaking suspense and intrigue! Does it make sense to you? Of course, what really matters is what the Bible teaches about Armageddon, wouldn't you say?

I have a number of doubts about Lindsey's scenario in *The Late Great Planet Earth*. For one thing, I can't accept his prediction that "the United States will cease being the leader of the West and will probably become in some way a part of the new European sphere of power." [2]

Bible prophecy teaches otherwise. The book of Revelation forecasts a powerful role for the United States in leading the world into earth's final crisis. For further study on America in prophecy you may want to read the chapter "Bloodstained

Stars and Stripes" in my book *The Rise and Fall of Antichrist.*

I have other concerns with *The Late Great Planet Earth*, some of them already covered in these pages. Nothing worries me more than the rapturists' teaching about a rebuilt Jewish temple in Jerusalem being the center of spiritual revival. Lindsey says that there will be a reinstitution of the Jewish worship according to the law of Moses with sacrifices and oblations.[3]

But tell me—wouldn't this compete with Calvary and deny the saving sacrifice of our Lord Jesus Christ? You will recall that when Jesus died, the veil of the temple tore apart, symbolizing the end of the Jewish temple services and sacrifices. Restoring those animal sacrifices would contradict what Christ has accomplished as the Lamb of God. And there's a word for that: it's called blasphemy.

Anything that competes with the finished sacrifice of Christ is the work of Satan, so *what would be so bad if the antichrist stopped those profane animal sacrifices? He would be doing a favor to the cause of Christ!*

I think you will agree that we are raising important questions here—questions that deeply concern anyone who appreciates Calvary as the complete and only sacrifice for sin.

Remember Daniel's prophecy foretelling the work of Jesus on the cross? Daniel said, "He shall bring an end to sacrifice and offering." Daniel 9:27. *Secret rapture teaching takes these beautiful words away from Christ and gives them to the antichrist!*

Now, I don't like to use strong language, so please understand that my conscience compels me to say this: It is nothing short of blasphemy to take Jesus out of Daniel 9:27 and replace Him with the antichrist. *This resurrects the most regrettable doctrine of the medieval Counter-Reformation and utterly undermines true Christian faith.*

Now, I *know* that rapturists trust in the blood of Jesus for their salvation, so why do they hope and pray that Jerusalem's temple will be rebuilt, anticipating that animal sacrifices will be offered on its altar? How can they consider such idolatry a spiritual revival? If the antichrist were to attack a rebuilt temple in Jerusalem and end its blasphemous sacrifices that denied the death of our Lord on Calvary, true Christians would have to call it the *blessing* of desolation, not the *abomination* of desolation!

*Think about that.*

Back in 1967, during the Six-Day War, the Israelis recaptured old Jerusalem. General Moshe Dayan marched to the wailing wall of the old temple and proclaimed, "We have returned to our holiest of holy places, never to leave her again." [4]

They returned to their holy place, but have they returned to their Messiah? Unfortunately, they have not. They still reject God's covenant of grace. So how can they consider themselves God's chosen people? The Bible clearly states that only "if you are Christ's, then you are Abraham's seed, and heirs according to the promise." Galatians 3:29.

Enlightened Bible scholars know that the Old Testament is not primarily *Israel*-centered, but *Messiah*-centered. The New Testament points us away from any temple on earth to heaven's sanctuary, where Jesus intercedes for us: "Now this is the main point of the things we are saying: We have such a High Priest, who is seated at the right hand of the throne of the Majesty in the heavens, a Minister of the sanctuary and of the true tabernacle which the Lord erected, and not man." Hebrews 8:1, 2.

You see, the true temple is in heaven now. The Lord built it, not man. Anything we built down here would be a counterfeit temple, and anything that would glorify the work of man by honoring such a false temple must be false teaching.

Nothing could be more clear than this: True prophecy points upward to heaven's temple in the New Jerusalem, while false prophecy points downward to an earthly temple in old Jerusalem.

All this talk about rebuilding the Jewish temple down

here—are we setting ourselves up for a counterfeit Armageddon? Jesus warned about false prophets with their false predictions concerning His coming. Could all the attention showered upon Israel be a smoke screen of the enemy to divert sincere Christians from the real issues of Armageddon?

I'm just asking questions here, but you might be interested to know that much of what rapturists teach about Jerusalem recycles what false prophets taught in Old Testament times. Six centuries before Christ, God's messenger Jeremiah predicted that unrepentant Jerusalem would fall prey to Babylon, while Hananiah, a popular religious teacher, opposed heaven's warning of doom. This false prophet assured the rebellious nation that they had nothing to worry about— God had already promised through Isaiah that He would bless Jerusalem, and that promise must stand, regardless of whether the nation repented.

Martin Buber, a modern Jewish theologian, shares some interesting insight into the situation just before the Babylonian invasion: "The false prophets popularized solely the promise of Isaiah's message, ignoring the condition inherent in each prophetic message of salvation; they changed the sure promise for an Israel that would faithfully fulfill her calling into an unconditional promise of security for all times."

In other words, false prophets in the Old Testament insisted that God would fulfill His covenant regardless of the way His people behaved. Do we hear echoes of the same teaching today?

Jeremiah faithfully rebuked the false prophets: "They continually say to those who despise Me, 'The Lord has said, "You shall have peace" '; and to everyone who walks according to the imagination of his own heart, 'No evil shall come upon you.' " Jeremiah 23:17.

Then the unpopular prophet of God warned the nation: "Your prophets have seen for you false and deceptive visions; they have not uncovered your iniquity, to bring back your captives, but have envisioned for you false prophecies and delusions." Lamentations 2:14.

So what made the difference between true and false prophecy in Israel's history? True prophets stressed that the nation must repent in order to receive the blessings of the covenant. False prophets taught that God would bless Jerusalem no matter what.

History was repeated in New Testament times. Just before the destruction of Jerusalem in A.D. 70, false prophets again arose, promising the Jews deliverance from enemy attacks. Josephus, the Jewish historian, reported how such false messengers encouraged presumptuous patriotism—until that final, fatal moment when the Roman army stormed Jerusalem. The unrepentant citizens perished with their false prophets.

Jesus warned the church to flee from the doomed city of Jerusalem. We would do well to take our Lord's advice today and flee from false prophecies about Jerusalem.

False faith in Jerusalem brought ruin in 605 B.C. and then again in A.D. 70. Will it happen again today? Something to consider carefully.

Then, what does the Bible mean by predicting the return of the Jews to Jerusalem? The answer comes very simply when we ask a further question: Where do God's people come out of when they return to Israel? *They come out of Babylon!* Here we have the key to understanding end-time Bible prophecy: The return of God's people to Jerusalem must be connected with Revelation's final warning, "Babylon the great is fallen. . . . Come out of her, my people." Revelation 18:2-4.

You see, when Old Testament prophets spoke of returning to Jerusalem they addressed the people of God captive in Babylon. The Jewish exiles had to leave Babylon in order to return to Jerusalem.

What does it mean for us today to "come out of Babylon"? That city doesn't even exist anymore. Visit the ancient site in

Iraq, as I have, and you will find only a pile of ruins.

So God's reference to modern Babylon cannot refer to a literal city. Is there some spiritual application for Babylon today?

Here's something interesting, something quite significant: The Reformers, all of them, taught that Babylon in the book of Revelation represents fallen Christianity—the church which had forsaken the faith of its first-century founders.

Were they correct? Does Babylon represent a corrupted Christianity which forfeits truth for the sake of false teachings? We must sadly acknowledge that many churches today have lost the prophetic faith of the Reformers. Many Protestants have adopted the falsehoods of the Counter-Reformation, that which their own founders condemned as the beliefs of Babylon.

For us, then, coming out of Babylon means exchanging such falsehood for the sake of truth, forsaking any thought that God's covenant of grace is being fulfilled to the Jewish nation outside of the blood of Jesus.

Returning to Jerusalem now means waiting by faith "for the city . . . whose builder and maker is God"—the New Jerusalem in heaven. Hebrews 11:10. Notice that the Lord is the builder of that celestial city, not an unbelieving Jewish architect in old Jerusalem. Our hope is not in "Jerusalem which now is, and is in bondage with her children—but the Jerusalem above is free, which is the mother of us all." Galatians 4:25, 26.

So we must look above us to the New Jerusalem, where Jesus intercedes as our High Priest in heaven's temple. We must depend on Him alone as our Saviour, our Lord, and our Coming King!

With all this in mind, we are now prepared to understand the battle of Armageddon.

Only one time does our Bible mention the word, in the book of Revelation: "They are the spirits of demons, performing signs, which go out to the kings of the earth and of the whole world, to gather them to the battle of that great day of God Almighty. . . . And they gathered them together to the place called in Hebrew, Armageddon." Revelation 16:14-16.

This "battle of that great day of God Almighty" is earth's final conflict. More than human forces will be fighting—the spiritual armies of God and Satan will clash. See Revelation 17:14. Armageddon climaxes the great controversy between good and evil.

Where will this battle be fought? History offers no record of any place called Armageddon, but the Bible gives us some hints. Our text says the word *Armageddon* comes from the Hebrew. In that language, the word combines *har,* which means "mountain," and *mageddon,* which many connect with Megiddo. So the name Armageddon can be understood as "mountain of Megiddo."

The mountain of Megiddo—here is a clue we can work with. Back in Old Testament times Megiddo was a small but important fortress city north of Jerusalem near the plain of Esdraelon. Once in Scripture this plain itself is called the plain of Megiddo. That might appear to be a logical location for warfare, but then we remember that Armageddon involves, not a plain, but a mountain.

We must find a *mountain* of Megiddo—a mountain with some spiritual significance for the armies of heaven.

Visiting the site of ancient Megiddo might help us understand Armageddon. We drive eastward from the Mediterranean port city of Haifa and follow the Carmel ridge. After passing the northeastern ridge of Carmel we locate the ruins of the ancient city. Looming large over the landscape at Megiddo is Mount Carmel. Maybe Mount Carmel solves our dilemma. Does it represent Mount Megiddo, the scene of Armageddon? Did something happen at Carmel that could help us understand Armageddon?

Long ago, Mount Carmel hosted a dramatic showdown between God and His enemies. The prophet Elijah summoned the nation to appear on the mountain. He challenged them to judge between true and false worship. Listen to his stirring appeal: "How long will you falter between two opinions? If the Lord is God, follow Him; but if Baal, then follow him." 1 Kings 18:21.

God won a great victory that day at Carmel. He defeated the enemies of His covenant, as He will again once for all at Armageddon.

*The New International Commentary on the New Testament* explains: "Har-Magedon is symbolic of the final overthrow of all the forces of evil by the might and power of God. . . . God will emerge victorious and take with him all who have placed their faith in him." [5]

So now we understand Armageddon. It's a showdown between truth and error, loyalty to God or to the powers of evil. While there certainly will be devastating battles among the armies of earth, the dominant theme of Scripture is that Armageddon centers around spiritual conflict.

And Armageddon involves every human being personally. To each of us comes the challenge, "How long will you falter between two opinions?" Will we come away from Babylon's falsehoods and obey God's covenant of grace? Will we be counted among the saints, who "keep the commandments of God and the faith of Jesus"? Revelation 14:12.

Yes, all of us have a part to play in Armageddon. When God overcomes the powers of evil, we can overcome with Him! Revelation assures us that the saints will triumphantly "sing the song of Moses, the servant of God, and the song of the Lamb." Revelation 15:3.

The song of Moses and the Lamb! What could this be?

Do you remember how God delivered Moses and the Israelites during their showdown with Pharaoh, during their Armageddon with its tribulation and its plagues? We too will endure tribulation during earth's last crisis. There will be "a time of trouble, such as never was since there was a nation, even to that time. And at that time your people shall be delivered." Daniel 12:1.

Thank God, He will deliver us, just as He saved Moses and the Israelites long ago. We will overcome earth's final tribulation through the blood of the Lamb—the blood of Jesus Christ on the doorposts of our hearts.

Imagine how thrilling it will be in heaven to stand before God's throne with the saints, that great multitude which no one can number. Clothed in white robes and holding palm branches of victory, we will break forth in joyous song: "Salvation belongs to our God . . . and to the Lamb!" Revelation 7:10.

I want to sing this song of Moses and the Lamb, don't you? It will be worth whatever it takes for us to come out of Babylon. Heaven will more than fulfill our fondest expectations!

Think about that day when the Lord Jesus Christ breaks through the eastern sky. Think about it over and over. Let it give you something to live for. Could anything be more exciting to contemplate?

Seeing first a small black cloud. Watching it move nearer and nearer till it becomes white and glorious. A cloud like none you've ever seen before—a cloud of angels, uncounted angels. Hearing a sound like none you've ever heard before—the sound of a trumpet echoing round the world. Then a voice like none you've heard before. It's the voice of our Lord calling the dead to life.

The earth quivers. Tombs burst open. Angels everywhere carry little children to their parents' eager arms. Loved ones long separated by death reunite with shouts of joy, never to part again! And then, together with those resurrected ones, we who have waited through earth's long night are caught up into that angel starship for the trip to our heavenly home.

I want to be there, and I know you do too! God help us be ready for that great day.

---

1. Lindsey, *Planet Earth,* p. 151.

2. *Ibid.*, p. 84.
3. *Ibid.*, p. 46.
4. *Ibid.*, p. 45.
5. *The Book of Revelation*, New International Commentary on the New Testament (Grand Rapids, Mich.: Eerdmans Publishing Co., 1977), p. 302. Quoted in Hans K. LaRondelle, *Chariots of Salvation* (Hagerstown, Md.: Review and Herald Publishing Association, 1987), p. 123.